Harsh Lessons:
Iraq, Afghanistan and the Changing Character of War

Ben Barry

'The military lessons from the wars in Iraq and Afghanistan are salutary, but neither the American army nor the British has been particularly good at learning them. While he was still serving, Ben Barry was tasked with writing the report on those which the British Army should draw from Iraq, but it was not published. His book is therefore well informed as well as important. "Harsh Lessons", and indeed the whole process of lesson learning, is not just about raking over the coals of the past; it is also about digesting their implications for the future.'
Professor Sir Hew Strachan, Emeritus Fellow, All Souls College, Oxford University, and Professor of International Relations, University of St Andrews

'Ben Barry has very aptly brought out the dynamics of the complexities and the changing character of conflict in the wars in Iraq and Afghanistan. The "harsh lesson" that all armies need to learn is that inadequate leadership – be it at the national or military level – coupled with the failure to expeditiously adapt to unforeseen circumstances can lead to defeat. To win future wars – be they hybrid, asymmetric, intra-state or inter-state, or fighting cross-border terrorism – a successful politico-military strategy will be one that harmonises all elements of national power and which is regularly assessed and reviewed.'
Lieutenant-General (Retd) P.K. Singh, former General Officer Commanding-in-Chief, South Western Command, Indian Army

Harsh Lessons:
Iraq, Afghanistan and the Changing Character of War

Ben Barry

IISS The International Institute for Strategic Studies

The International Institute for Strategic Studies

Arundel House | 13–15 Arundel Street | Temple Place | London | WC2R 3DX | UK

First published January 2017 **Routledge**
4 Park Square, Milton Park, Abingdon, Oxon, OX14 4RN

for **The International Institute for Strategic Studies**
Arundel House, 13–15 Arundel Street, Temple Place, London, WC2R 3DX, UK
www.iiss.org

Simultaneously published in the USA and Canada by **Routledge**
270 Madison Ave., New York, NY 10016

Routledge is an imprint of Taylor & Francis, an Informa Business

© 2017 The International Institute for Strategic Studies

DIRECTOR-GENERAL AND CHIEF EXECUTIVE Dr John Chipman
EDITOR Dr Nicholas Redman
EDITORIAL Jeffrey Mazo, Chris Raggett, Jill Lally, Alice Aveson
COVER/PRODUCTION John Buck, Kelly Verity
COVER IMAGE An Iraqi boy taunts British soldiers during an incident in Basra,
19 September 2005 (Reuters/Atef Hassan).

The International Institute for Strategic Studies is an independent centre for research, information and debate on the problems of conflict, however caused, that have, or potentially have, an important military content. The Council and Staff of the Institute are international and its membership is drawn from almost 100 countries. The Institute is independent and it alone decides what activities to conduct. It owes no allegiance to any government, any group of governments or any political or other organisation. The IISS stresses rigorous research with a forward-looking policy orientation and places particular emphasis on bringing new perspectives to the strategic debate.

The Institute's publications are designed to meet the needs of a wider audience than its own membership and are available on subscription, by mail order and in good bookshops. Further details at www.iiss.org.

British Library Cataloguing in Publication Data
A catalogue record for this book is available from the British Library

Library of Congress Cataloging in Publication Data

ADELPHI series
ISSN 1944-5571

ADELPHI 461
ISBN 978-1-138-06096-8

Contents

For Lance Corporal Paul Thomas, Second Battalion the Light Infantry, Rifleman Jamie Gunn, First Battalion the Rifles, Lieutenant Colonel Rupert Thorneloe, First Battalion the Welsh Guards, and Sir Hilary Synnott, HM Diplomatic Service and IISS. They all marched to the sound of the guns.

ACKNOWLEDGEMENTS

My final job in the British Army was writing a report on the lessons learned from stabilisation operations in Iraq. Originally restricted, it was declassified in 2016.[1] Since October 2010, when I joined the IISS, I have been analysing the continuing wars in Iraq and Afghanistan.

Many of the ideas expressed in this book have already been aired in other IISS publications: *Survival*, *Strategic Survey* and *The Military Balance*. I am grateful to the editors of all three: Dana Allin, Alexander Nicoll, Nicholas Redman and James Hackett. I would particularly like to thank my IISS colleagues: General (Retd) Lord David Richards, Lieutenant-General H.R. McMaster, Nigel Inkster, Professor Toby Dodge, Douglas Barrie, Professor Sir Hew Strachan, Desmond Bowen, Philip Barton, Jack Baker, Maxime Humeau, Michael Tong and the IISS's excellent librarians. Special thanks are due to Lieutenant-General (Retd) Dick Applegate and General Sir Nick Carter for sponsoring field trips to Afghanistan, and to Colonel (Retd) Alexander Alderson, PhD for mentoring my research on Iraq.

GLOSSARY

ANSF	Afghan National Security Forces
CENTCOM	US Central Command
CFC–A	Combined Forces Command–Afghanistan
CJTF-7	Combined Joint Task Force 7
COIN	Counter-insurgency
CPA	Coalition Provisional Authority
EFP	Explosively formed projectile
EOD	Explosive-ordnance disposal
F3EAD	Find, fix, finish, exploit, analyse and disseminate
FCO	Foreign and Commonwealth Office
HUMINT	Human Intelligence
IED	Improvised explosive device
ISAF	International Security Assistance Force
ISF	Iraqi Security Forces
ISTAR	Information, surveillance, target acquisition and reconnaissance
JAM	Jaish al-Mahdi
JSOC	Joint Special Operations Command
LAV	Light armoured vehicle
MiTT	Military Transition Team
MNF–I	Multi-National Force–Iraq
MoD	Ministry of Defence (UK)
MRAP	Mine-resistant ambush-protected vehicle
OMLT	Operational Mentor and Liaison Team

ORHA   Office for Reconstruction and Humanitarian Assistance

PRT   Provincial Reconstruction Team

RMA   Revolution in Military Affairs

SOCOM   Special Operations Command

SOF   Special-operations forces

SOFA   Status of Forces Agreement

UAV   Unmanned aerial vehicle

UGV   Unmanned ground vehicle

USAF   United States Air Force

USMC   US Marine Corps

Prussian military theorist Carl von Clausewitz outlined two facets of war: its nature, which remains constant under all circumstances; and its character, which encompasses the varying ways and means by which war is fought. War's nature is inherently human, often chaotic. Waging war is an act or expression of policy, undertaken to maintain a position of advantage, create a more advantageous situation or influence the attitudes or behaviour of another party. The measure of a war's success is the extent to which belligerents deem its political outcomes to be favourable. Opponents may employ all the military and non-military ways and means available to them to seek success.

War is a dynamic activity in which opponents constantly seek an advantage over one another. Effective use of new technology or tactics by one actor usually results in attempts by its opponents to develop countermeasures. If successful, these countermeasures often prompt further adaptation by the enemy. Therefore, most wars feature complex action–reaction dynamics that constantly change their character.

The post-9/11 wars in Iraq and Afghanistan have dominated the experience of US and allied land and air forces this century. These forces have changed a great deal as a result of this experience – as much as they did in either world war in the twentieth century.

The aim of this *Adelphi* book is to analyse the changing character of conflict in the wars in Iraq and Afghanistan, with a view to identifying pointers to the future character of conflict. Analysing the wars from a military perspective, it seeks to give readers a clear understanding of the ways in which the character of both conflicts changed. The book examines strategic, operational, tactical and technical adaptations and adjustments during the wars to show how strategy, campaign design and military capability evolved. This allows readers to identify the elements of these factors that have a wider application.

The wars began with the al-Qaeda attacks on the United States on 11 September 2001. American combat troops left Iraq in December 2011, and the US-led NATO combat mission in Afghanistan ended in December 2014. Thirteen years of fighting led to more than 35,000 casualties among American and allied forces, and around 250,000 civilian casualties; the US alone required more than US$1.5 trillion in additional military funding over and above the Pentagon's annual budget.

In both Iraq and Afghanistan, the US and its allies came extremely close to strategic defeat, due to inadequate leadership, reconstruction efforts, political strategy, military strategy, operational concepts, tactics and equipment. These shortfalls combined with failures – at every level – to adapt quickly enough to unforeseen circumstances, and provided opportunities that were exploited by insurgents and militias.

In both wars, it took several years for the US and its allies to recognise that the ends, ways and means they employed were insufficient for the task. Although they eventually adapted to provide enough security for limited political progress, the widespread perception that the conflicts were intractable, and the difficulty of achieving strategic success, resulted in a loss of confidence in the West in the utility of force as an instrument of state power. The political and military credibility of the US and its allies was damaged.

The wars in Iraq and Afghanistan have been described by many journalists. There is no shortage of memoirs. But there has been much less discussion of how the character of the wars evolved, and of the implications of these developments for armed conflict and armed forces in the future. To understand this evolution, a frame of reference is needed – a baseline idea of the likely future character of conflict. This would allow judgements to be made about the potential utility of specific ways and means of war.

According to the IISS Armed Conflict Database, since 9/11, the overwhelming majority of armed conflicts have been intra-state. The IISS *Armed Conflict Survey 2016* confirms that the trend is continuing, and will most likely do so throughout 2017 and beyond. Post-9/11 armed conflict between states includes US-led regime change in Afghanistan and Iraq, the 2008 Russia–Georgia War and Russia's 2014 annexation of Crimea and sponsorship of rebel factions in eastern Ukraine. Israel's 2006 conflict with Hizbullah and wars with Hamas in Gaza involved non-state actors with many of the characteristics of states. And the NATO intervention in Libya in 2011 had much of the character of a war to support rebel groups fighting against the Gadhafi regime.

Although inter-state wars have been in the minority since 9/11, there are many potential flashpoints for further such conflicts in the Middle East and Asia. These include tension between Pakistan and India, the two Koreas, and Iran and its neighbours, as well as China's unresolved maritime disputes in the South and East China seas.

The future is likely to see constant intra-state conflict, including terrorism, insurgencies and civil wars. Hybrid conflicts may combine some or all of these traits with elements of inter-

Key terminology: levels of war

The military forces of NATO, the US and most other Western countries use the concept of levels of warfare to express the way in which war is planned and conducted. The terms are used extensively in this book. These simplified definitions are based on current US joint doctrine.[1]

Strategic level: At this level, a nation often determines the national (or multinational, in the case of an alliance or coalition) guidance that addresses strategic objectives in support of strategic end states and develops and uses national resources to achieve them.

Operational level: This level links strategy and tactics by establishing the objectives needed to achieve the military end states and strategic objectives. It sequences tactical actions to achieve objectives. At this level, the focus is on the planning and execution of operations using operational art: the cognitive approach by commanders and their staff (supported by their skill, knowledge, experience, creativity and judgement) to develop strategies, campaigns and operations to organise and employ military forces by integrating ends, ways and means. The operational level has been described by General David Richards as

the vital gearing between tactical activity and the strategic level at which politicians and Chiefs of Defence operate. It is the level at which campaigns are run and where political intent is analysed and turned into military effect; it is where wars are won or lost and it is demanding stuff.[2]

Tactical level: Tactics is the employment and ordered arrangement of forces in relation to each other. This level of war is where battles and engagements are planned and executed to achieve military objectives assigned to tactical units.

Campaigns: A campaign is a series of related major operations aimed at achieving strategic and operational objectives within a given time and space.

Operations: An operation is a sequence of tactical actions with a common purpose or unifying theme. An operation may entail the process of carrying on combat, including the movement, supply, attack, defence and manoeuvres needed to achieve the objective of any battle or campaign. A major operation is a series of tactical actions – such as battles, engagements and strikes – conducted by combat forces coordinated in time and space to achieve strategic or operational objectives.

In reality, the boundaries between the levels of war often blur and shift. And events may have simultaneous implications at all three levels.

state conflict. But the potential for inter-state conflict remains, carrying with it the risk of escalation in time, space, intensity, casualties and displacement of civilians. This provides the framework for assessing pointers to the future character of conflict.

The US provided most of the forces involved in the wars in Iraq and Afghanistan. The United Kingdom also played a key role, as one of the two 'occupying powers' in Iraq in 2003–04 and as the second-largest contributor of troops to both wars. There is an abundance of US primary-source documents for both wars. The UK's Iraq Inquiry provides a cornucopia of testimony by politicians, officials and military officers that illuminates the higher management of the war. I do not ignore other countries that contributed forces, but the US and UK military experience makes up the bulk of this book.

Given the length of the wars, the hundreds of thousands of US and allied personnel involved and the millions of people who lived through the fighting, this analysis is highly selective. The book does not cover the flawed assessments of Iraq's weapons-of-mass-destruction capability made by US, UK and other intelligence agencies, nor the political and diplomatic processes that led to the UK and US decisions to attack Iraq. An analysis that does justice to these important topics would require another *Adelphi*.

This book analyses the wars from a military perspective, focusing on issues of the greatest enduring military importance. It assesses the management of reconstruction and the integration of civilian and military efforts, but not the reconstruction effort itself. Other excluded topics include force preparation and training, sea power, police capacity-building, logistics and military mental health.

CHAPTER ONE

The changing character of the conflicts

As the character of the wars in Afghanistan and Iraq shifted from regime change to prolonged counter-insurgency campaigns, they became increasingly political, even at the tactical level. Sometimes described as 'armed politics', these dynamics were heavily influenced by the battle of the narrative. This contest focused on influencing attitudes and involved insurgent and militia propaganda, international forces' information operations and statements by a wide variety of political and military leaders.

In 1991 *Operation Desert Storm* saw a US-led coalition eject the Iraqi Army from Kuwait. In 1995 UN and NATO air and artillery strikes helped end the war in Bosnia. In 1999 a US-led NATO air campaign forced the withdrawal of Serb troops from Kosovo. After both Balkan campaigns, NATO troops successfully enforced post-conflict security. All these operations succeeded, and international forces incurred few casualties during them. They were supported by their countries' politicians, public and media. But the Bosnian and Serb forces were often unwilling to stand and fight, and were overmatched by NATO's modern combat capabilities and superior training.

In September 2001, the forces of the US and its allies were confident that they could conduct challenging peace-support operations. Many armed forces, defence manufacturers and theorists believed in the concept of the Revolution in Military Affairs (RMA). Advocates of the RMA claimed that greatly improved surveillance, communications and precision-strike weapons would produce superior knowledge of the enemy and better-targeted and more effective strikes and manoeuvre, allowing a modernised and networked force to defeat a larger but less modernised one.

The government of US President George W. Bush, who was inaugurated in January 2001, considered operations such as those in the Balkans and the 1994–95 intervention in Haiti to have fixed the US military in open-ended commitments that significantly reduced strategic flexibility. As a result, the administration sought to reduce the use of US military forces for nation building and to make them more flexible, deployable and responsive – by fully exploiting the RMA.

After the Taliban government in Kabul refused to expel al-Qaeda and hand over Osama bin Laden in the wake of 9/11, the US faced the unforeseen requirement of having to attack Afghanistan. Washington developed a plan in which CIA teams would arm and fund the anti-Taliban Northern Alliance militias, with US special-operations forces (SOF) linking up with the CIA and the Northern Alliance to coordinate supporting airstrikes. US ground troops would be introduced to complete the destruction of the Taliban and al-Qaeda. Once this was complete, there would be stabilisation operations.

As the US and the UK launched *Operation Enduring Freedom* on 7 October 2001, attacking Taliban forces with missiles and bombs, Northern Alliance militias began their offensive. The SOF directed precision airstrikes, multiplying the combat power of the anti-Taliban forces. As Afghan cities fell to the

Northern Alliance, many surviving Taliban fighters, including their leader, Mullah Omar, fled to Pakistan.[1]

From March 2002 onwards, the majority of US government and military attention switched from stabilising Afghanistan to planning the attack on Iraq. Afghanistan became a strategic 'economy of force' operation. In May 2003, US Secretary of Defense Donald Rumsfeld told journalists that in Afghanistan 'we're at a point where we clearly have moved from major combat activity to a period of stability and stabilization and reconstruction activities'.[2]

Before 9/11, the US had a military plan for an attack on Iraq. It envisaged a force of 400,000 troops assembling over time. The unexpectedly rapid US success in Afghanistan prompted General Tommy Franks, commander of US Central Command (CENTCOM), to develop a plan that could be implemented more quickly. It emphasised surprise and speed of manoeuvre, reducing the number of troops required:

> Our ground forces, supported by overwhelming air power, would move so fast and deep into the Iraqi rear that time-and-distance factors would preclude the enemy's defensive manoeuvre. And this slow-reacting enemy would be fixed in place by the combined effect of artillery, air support, and attack helicopters ... We would not apply overwhelming force. Rather, we would apply the overwhelming 'mass of effect' of a smaller force. Speed would represent a mass all its own.[3]

The plan was executed largely as Franks intended. In 2003 around 170,000 troops – most of them American, and the remainder British or Australian – took part in the invasion of Iraq. They achieved a degree of surprise through the near-simultaneous start of ground and air offensives rather than a long air campaign of the kind that US-led forces had employed in *Operation Desert Storm* in 1991. *Operation Iraqi Freedom* displayed an impressive degree of air–land synergy, in which precision attack and rapid manoeuvre by well-equipped and -trained land and air forces led to an even more decisive defeat of the Iraqi military than had occurred in 1991.[4] On 1 May, Bush declared the end of major combat operations while standing on the deck of the aircraft carrier USS *Abraham Lincoln*, beneath a banner reading 'mission accomplished'.

The Afghanistan War

The December 2001 Bonn Agreement, brokered between prominent Afghan leaders by the United Nations, saw Hamid Karzai appointed as interim Afghan president, and established a committee to draft a new constitution. International donors pledged billions of dollars in aid to support reconstruction, development, counter-narcotics programmes and the formation of new security forces in Afghanistan. There was to be an international effort to conduct security-sector reform. Around 10,000 US and Coalition troops remained in the country to neutralise al-Qaeda and Taliban forces. Wherever intelligence indicated promising targets, US forces launched search-and-destroy missions against the remnants of al-Qaeda and the Taliban. While these attacks were sometimes successful, the resulting civilian casualties and collateral damage increasingly alienated Afghan civilians.

At the same time, the UK assembled the International Security Assistance Force (ISAF). This was a multinational infantry brigade (later under NATO command) deployed by air to support the Afghan authorities in maintaining security in Kabul, as envisaged by the Bonn Agreement and established by a UN Security Council resolution.

In 2003 a new US-led theatre command for Afghanistan was formed: Combined Forces Command–Afghanistan (CFC–A). To assist the Afghan authorities and the UN, CFC–A commander Lieutenant-General David Barno developed a fresh concept for Coalition operations, at the centre of which was an inter-agency counter-insurgency (COIN) approach.

Barno allocated responsibility for all regions of Afghanistan to US military commanders. Conventional forces would cease their episodic deployment for search-and-destroy raids. Instead, they would be assigned to specific Afghan provinces. Most US troops were based in southern and eastern Afghanistan, where the al-Qaeda and Taliban threat was greatest.

In January 2004, the new constitution was adopted; the following October, Karzai was elected president. The international community agreed on very ambitious long-term targets for reconstruction, development and reform, particularly that of the Afghan army and police. The Karzai government's authority was weak outside Kabul, and it often relied on the co-option and empowerment of local strongmen and militia warlords. These figures, as well as the underdeveloped and undertrained Afghan National Security Forces (ANSF), often preyed on local civilians.

The Taliban reconstituted its political and military capabilities. The group infiltrated Afghanistan from Pakistan, rebuilding its military and political networks. It exploited widespread discontent with government officials' corruption and acts of extortion, as well as Afghan civilian deaths caused by US and Coalition forces. Attacks against the ANSF and government targets gradually increased.

In 2006 the US reduced its forces in Afghanistan to reinforce Iraq, and ISAF assumed responsibility for stabilising the whole country. British General David Richards, the new ISAF commander, formulated a COIN campaign plan that also sought to support and empower the Afghan authorities. To better coordinate Afghan and international efforts, a policy action group chaired by Karzai acted as a top-level committee. The Coalition conducted military operations to secure Afghan Development Zones. A force made up of Canadian, Dutch and UK troops was tasked with securing key areas for reconstruction and development in southern Afghanistan.

But the Taliban was much stronger in southern Afghanistan than expected, leading to intense fighting in which British troops only held their positions through the heavy use of airpower, resulting in collateral damage and civilian casualties. Coupled with an inadequate understanding of local cultural, political

Counter-insurgency (COIN) doctrine in Iraq and Afghanistan

After the Vietnam War, the US Army had deliberately neglected training and education in COIN. The US marines retained an interest in 'small wars', not least because they regarded some of their stability operations in Vietnam as successes.

However, some US Army and Marine officers quickly realised that the Afghan and Iraq wars were both insurgencies, requiring a COIN approach. Lieutenant-General David Barno adopted this approach in Afghanistan in 2003, and COIN thinking greatly informed 2004 planning by the marines before they assumed responsibility for Iraq's Anbar Province. The marines and the army both used COIN approaches to clear Al-Qaim and Tal Afar.

US thinking about COIN reached critical mass in 2006, when General David Petraeus and Marine General James Mattis applied their considerable operational experience and intellectual energy to developing a new doctrine for COIN. A new COIN field manual published at the end of 2006 drew not only on the emerging lessons of Iraq and Afghanistan, but also on a historical analysis of successful and failed COIN campaigns. The manual's key points were that:

Military efforts are necessary and important to [COIN] efforts, but they are only effective when integrated into a comprehensive strategy employing all instruments of national power. A successful COIN operation meets the contested population's needs to the extent needed to win popular support while protecting the population from the insurgents.

The integration of civilian and military efforts is crucial to successful COIN operations. All efforts focus on supporting the local populace and HN [host-nation] government. Political, social, and economic programs are usually more valuable than conventional military opera-

and tribal dynamics, this caused further deterioration of security in southern Afghanistan. In September 2006, Canadian, US and Afghan troops conducted *Operation Medusa*, attacking a Taliban force assembling near Kandahar for an assault on the city. This was NATO's first-ever brigade-level attack.[5]

Between 2006 and 2009, ISAF and the ANSF achieved a measure of stability in Kabul, as well as northern and western Afghanistan. But in the south and east, the Taliban's strength increased, despite ISAF repeatedly mounting offensive operations. These efforts usually succeeded in clearing insurgents, but the lack of sufficient NATO or Afghan troops meant that international forces could not hold these areas and had to

tions in addressing the root causes of conflict and undermining an insurgency.

An essential COIN task for military forces is fighting insurgents; however, these forces can and should use their capabilities to meet the local populace's fundamental needs as well. Regaining the populace's active and continued support for the HN government is essential to deprive an insurgency of its power and appeal. The military forces' primary function in COIN is protecting that populace. However, employing military force is not the only way to provide civil security or defeat insurgents. Indeed, excessive use of military force can frequently undermine policy objectives at the expense of achieving the overarching political goals that define success. This dilemma places tremendous importance on the measured application of force.

Durable policy success requires balancing the measured use of force with an emphasis on nonmilitary programs. Political, social, and economic programs are most commonly and appropriately associated with civilian organizations and expertise; however, effective implementation of these programs is more important than who performs the tasks. If adequate civilian capacity is not available, military forces fill the gap.

COIN is also a battle of ideas. Insurgents seek to further their cause by creating misperceptions of COIN efforts. Comprehensive information programs are necessary to amplify the messages of positive deeds and to counter insurgent propaganda.[6]

The manual also systematised the 'clear, hold, build' approach applied in Tal Afar. It became extremely influential, greatly informing the training and approach of US and allied forces in Iraq and Afghanistan from 2007 onwards.

withdraw. As well as causing civilian casualties and collateral damage, these operations exposed Afghan civilians who had supported their government to Taliban retaliation after the withdrawal of Coalition troops. NATO commanders came to call this approach 'mowing the lawn'. The Alliance was failing to make security gains sufficient to wrest the strategic initiative from the insurgents. Meanwhile, unexpectedly heavy casualties reduced the popularity of the war in NATO nations.

In March 2009, newly elected US president Barack Obama despatched an additional 17,000 US troops to Afghanistan. In a report completed in August 2009, the new ISAF commander, US General Stanley McChrystal, recommended the implementation of a comprehensive COIN campaign, applying relevant lessons from Iraq. This would require an additional 40,000 US troops. His report was leaked, sparking intense political and media speculation that damaged civil–military relations in Washington. In December 2009, Obama announced that 30,000 US troops would be sent to Afghanistan, with NATO invited to make up the difference. US objectives were to deny a safe haven to al-Qaeda and reverse Taliban momentum, preventing it from overthrowing the Afghan government. But the surge was to be time-limited, and to remain at its peak strength for only 18 months. Subsequently, the US and NATO agreed that ISAF's combat role would end by 2015.

McChrystal assessed that the conflict's centre of gravity was the Afghan population, which had to be protected from the insurgents and ISAF firepower. This 'courageous-restraint' approach was implemented through more restrictive rules of engagement. He sought to separate the Afghan people from the insurgents; improve their security, governance and economic prospects; and degrade insurgent capabilities. The military's role included clearing the main populated areas of insurgents, conducting targeted raids to capture or kill insurgent leaders, developing the ANSF and supporting the development of Afghan governance.

ISAF's main task was to extend Afghan government control over heavily populated areas in Helmand and Kandahar provinces. Cleared territory was to be held. The campaign began in February 2010 with *Operation Moshtarak*, which involved US, UK and Afghan forces in Helmand Province. The resilience of the insurgents, who fought back after the initial assault, showed that in 'clear, hold, build' operations, the second phase could be more difficult than the first. But the operation led to a significant improvement in security in central Helmand. In June 2010, the main effort switched to *Operation Hamkari*, designed to clear Kandahar city and surrounding districts. Heavy fighting by US, Canadian and Afghan troops cleared and held the districts of Panjwai, Zhari and Arghandab.[7]

ISAF's understanding of the complex Afghan environment had greatly improved since 2006, as had its intelligence-gathering capabilities. Large numbers of surveillance systems and SOF were redeployed by the US from Iraq to Afghanistan. In December 2010, ISAF reached its peak strength of 131,000 troops. In May 2011, US SOF flew from Afghanistan to raid Osama bin Laden's hideout in Pakistan, resulting in his death. In June 2011, Obama announced that the surge had peaked and troop levels would decline.

Over the following three years, areas cleared by ISAF and Afghan forces were generally held and the leadership of operations gradually passed to Afghan forces as ISAF reduced its numbers. Pro-government forces defeated persistent Taliban efforts to regain control of cleared areas, but the insurgents continued to occasionally mount high-profile attacks in Kabul, all of which were contained and countered by Afghan police. The Afghan authorities and security forces managed two successive rounds of presidential elections in

2014. Ashraf Ghani became president under a power-sharing deal with his opponent Abdullah Abdullah. All Afghan provinces transitioned to Afghan security leadership by June 2014. ISAF casualties declined as those among the ANSF increased.

By 2015, US and NATO troops had withdrawn from combat missions. NATO began *Operation Resolute Support* to train, advise and assist Afghan forces, while a US-led counter-terrorism mission was tasked with attacking al-Qaeda and its affiliates. The ANSF had largely reached its planned strength of 352,000, but it still relied on NATO for artillery support and airstrikes, airborne intelligence gathering and help in operating medical and logistic/administrative systems. NATO's training mission concentrated on building capacity in these areas; strengthening medical, counter-improvised-explosive-device and intelligence capabilities; and developing the institutional capacity of the defence and interior ministries.

There was heavy fighting in Afghanistan in 2015, resulting in more Afghan military and civilian casualties than ever before. Although the ANSF retained control of most key populated areas, it continued to display weaknesses in leadership, command, control and coordination. The Taliban exploited these shortfalls in an attack in which it captured Kunduz, holding the city for two weeks. Overall ANSF attrition levels were higher than expected.[8] Obama subsequently announced that US troops would remain in Afghanistan after 2016.

The Iraq War

The nearest thing to a unified Coalition declaration of strategic objectives in Iraq was the Azores Statement by President Bush, UK Prime Minister Tony Blair and Spanish Prime Minister José Maria Aznar in March 2003. The leaders stated:

We will work to prevent and repair damage by
Saddam Hussein's regime to the natural resources of
Iraq and pledge to protect them as a national asset of
and for the Iraqi people. All Iraqis should share the
wealth generated by their national economy ... In
achieving this vision, we plan to work in close part-
nership with international institutions, including the
United Nations ... Any military presence, should
it be necessary, will be temporary and intended to
promote security and elimination of weapons of mass
destruction; the delivery of humanitarian aid; and the
conditions for the reconstruction of Iraq.[9]

US planning for post-conflict stabilisation and reconstruction lagged behind military planning for regime change. The
decision to assign responsibility for post-conflict stabilisation
to the Department of Defense was not taken until early 2003,
when the Pentagon established the Office for Reconstruction
and Humanitarian Assistance (ORHA). The Pentagon planned
to assign international advisers to Iraqi government ministries
and to recall the surviving units of the Iraqi army to maintain
order.

These plans were rapidly overtaken by events. Iraq's infrastructure was in a far worse state than the US expected. Many
members of the Iraqi security forces demobilised without fighting, partly as a result of US information operations. Too few
Coalition forces had been allocated to provide security. The
vacuum was filled by criminals, insurgents and sectarian militias, creating a climate of lawlessness.

The ORHA struggled to meet the reconstruction challenge.
Less than two months after the invasion began, it was replaced
with the Coalition Provisional Authority (CPA), headed by Paul
Bremer, a US diplomat with little background in the Middle

East, reconstruction or development. In May 2003, the CPA decreed that the Iraqi security forces would be disbanded and the top four tiers of Ba'ath Party members removed from public positions. This immediately destroyed any remaining Iraqi governance and law-and-order capability, making stabilisation and reconstruction much more difficult. These decisions, and the rapid handover of responsibility for de-Ba'athification to a cabal of Shia politicians, increased the alienation of Iraq's disenfranchised Sunni minority. The CPA succeeded in issuing a new currency, forming an advisory Iraq Governing Council, preparing for elections and arranging the formation of an interim Iraqi government. But hard-pressed military commanders often saw little value in the authority's activities.[10]

Three separate insurgencies arose, with a shared aim of ejecting Coalition forces: elements of the former regime began to conduct guerrilla warfare and terrorist attacks; disenfranchised Sunnis formed a self-organising insurgency; and large numbers of al-Qaeda fighters flowed across the Iraq–Syria border, initially with direct assistance from the Syrian government. By 2004 there was a large-scale insurgency in Sunni areas.

Coalition forces lacked the strength to provide security but had enough troops to be seen by the Iraqi people as occupiers. Civilian casualties, a lack of intelligence and inadequate cultural awareness meant that security operations often antagonised and humiliated ordinary Iraqis, further undermining the legitimacy of the Coalition. This was exacerbated by the April 2004 publication and widespread dissemination of photographs of US troops abusing prisoners at Abu Ghraib, a former regime prison that the Coalition turned into a detention centre.

The endemic lawlessness and rapid organisation by Shia parties led to a growth of Shia militias, including Moqtada al-Sadr's Jaish al-Mahdi (JAM) and the Iranian-supported Badr Brigade. The Coalition, Iraqi authorities and emerging Iraqi security forces struggled to counter them. Organised crime prospered, with gangs often overmatching the embryonic Iraqi police forces. Insecurity and the deterioration of public services, especially the electricity supply, eroded support for the Coalition among the Iraqi people. Insurgents and militias attacked political and religious rivals, as well as Iraqis who worked for the Coalition and emerging state institutions.

The Pentagon seems to have originally anticipated that post-conflict stabilisation would be relatively undemanding. Instead, it quickly became a bloody war in a broken country against enemies who stood their ground, fought and died. Failure to find weapons of mass destruction, the abuse of prisoners, the rising toll of military and civilian casualties and a rapidly deteriorating security situation eroded public support in nations contributing troops to the Coalition. Between 2004 and 2007, the insurgents and militias had the initiative. They ruthlessly exploited the internet and satellite television to disseminate their message, using the 'propaganda of the deed' as an integral part of their tactics and strategy.

The US adopted a transition strategy in which responsibility for security would be transferred to the Iraqis as quickly as possible. This was to be implemented by building the Iraqi Security Forces (ISF) and withdrawing US troops from urban areas to a few large bases on the edges of Iraqi towns and cities. In May 2004, the Coalition military command, organised as Combined Joint Task Force 7, was restructured, becoming the Multi-National Force–Iraq (MNF–I). In June 2004, the CPA was disbanded and sovereignty passed to an interim Iraqi administration. Elections held in January and December 2005 were successful, in part because all major Shia actors saw them as an opportunity. Many Sunnis boycotted the votes.

There was the appearance of political progress. Elections for a Transitional National Assembly, a referendum on a constitution and parliamentary elections (all in 2005), and the success of Iraqi forces' contribution to security operations, led to optimism in Washington and London. But the May 2006 formation of a Shia-dominated government under Prime Minister Nuri al-Maliki of the Shia Dawa Party undermined the confidence of the increasingly discontented Sunni minority. Maliki was supported by the US and personally mentored by Bush.

Between 2004 and 2006, the US failed to adequately strengthen the capability of Iraqi forces and neutralise the Sunni and al-Qaeda insurgencies – except in the towns of Al-Qaim and Tal Afar, where sufficient US and Iraqi forces conducted successful 'clear, hold, build' COIN operations. The stabilisation of Tal Afar by Colonel H.R. McMaster's 3rd Armoured Cavalry Regiment was particularly influential. The city was systematically cleared in a carefully sequenced operation. Patrol bases were built to dominate all the main routes. Fighting was intense, but use of US heavy weapons was carefully controlled. The regiment recruited and trained 1,400 Iraqi police to build legitimacy and partner US units. The MNF–I persuaded the Iraqi government to lead on the public presentation of the operation. Popular consent was obtained by re-establishing essential services and by targeted reconstruction efforts. As popular support for US and Iraqi forces increased, it generated intelligence that could be exploited for further attacks on insurgents.

Sectarian strife between Iraq's Shi'ites and Sunnis was inflamed by al-Qaeda, especially by the February 2006 bombing of the Samarra mosque. The country descended into ethnic cleansing and a sectarian civil war, a self-reinforcing cycle of atrocity and reprisal. Throughout 2006, repeated US-led military efforts to stabilise the deteriorating situation in Baghdad failed. As Maliki initially depended on the parliamentary votes of Shia political parties that sponsored militias, he was unwilling to challenge Shia extremists.

But, in Ramadi, a US brigade successfully applied a COIN approach. As US troops cleared the town, they were approached by Sunni tribes that wanted to fight al-Qaeda. The US supported them with its firepower and incorporated them into its operations, starting the 'Anbar Awakening'. This was a tipping point (although it was not widely recognised as such at the time).

In late 2006, Bush personally reviewed the war. He rejected advice from the Washington security establishment to continue with the transition strategy. Drawing on outside advice, he ordered a surge of extra troops to create sufficient security and the space for reconciliation and politics.

The surge in Iraq was explicitly designed as a COIN operation. US units were partnered with Iraqi units, constructing Joint Security Stations on key urban terrain. Once insurgent and militia activity had been reduced and the area broadly stabilised, it became possible for the increasingly capable and confident Iraqi forces, supported by embedded US mentors, to assume security responsibility for these areas, allowing US units to be redeployed for further clearance operations. Using the COIN approach that had worked in Al-Qaim, Tal Afar and Ramadi, General David Petraeus, the new commander of the MNF–I, attacked the Sunni–al-Qaeda insurgency and Shia militias in key areas of Baghdad. Petraeus also directed US troops to embrace the Anbar Awakening. By mid-2008, around 100,000 irregulars had been added to the US government payroll as 'Sons of Iraq', putting four times as many additional boots on the ground as had been sent to Iraq by the surge.

This allowed the US to change the character of the conflict to successful 'clear, hold, build' COIN operations that protected the Iraqi people. The surge reversed the deteriorating security situation, exploiting and reinforcing the growing capability and confidence of the ISF. However, while surge operations challenged Shia militias in key areas of Baghdad, the US did not contest the groups' control of Sadr City, a million-strong suburb. By early 2008, the US had begun to reduce troop numbers again, effectively resuming the transition strategy.

The British in the south

Southern Iraq (with its predominantly Shia population) and Basra (Iraq's second city and only port) were the responsibility of a British-led multinational division. UK force levels declined after May 2003, and fell further after London decided in 2004 to commit a major force to Afghanistan.

After the 2005 elections, the UK expected that there would be political and security progress in southern Iraq. Instead, elected local politicians all strongly opposed the British presence, and by 2006 the transition strategy was failing in the region. Local politicians and Iraqi forces were unwilling to confront Shia militias, which sought to gain political capital by attacking the British. Roadside bomb attacks by Shia militants sharply increased British casualties.

As UK public support for the war was decreasing with every casualty, the British declined to match the January 2007 US surge. London argued that Basra's Shia majority made the city different from the rest of the country, and that previous efforts to stabilise it had failed to change its political dynamic. The British felt that, as they were losing legitimacy, it was now up to the Iraqi government and security forces to take the lead. Due to commitments to build up forces in Afghanistan, the British were unable to send reinforcements to Iraq. Instead, UK forces withdrew from Basra as part of an 'accommodation' with Shia militias, under which the latter temporarily ceased their attacks on the British. This led to the imposition of a hard-line Islamist regime in Basra, and organised crime flourished.

In 2008 Shia political dynamics changed. Maliki became less dependent on the parliamentary votes of Sadrists, who were strongly linked with the Basra militias. In late March, Maliki surprised both Petraeus and the British by suddenly announcing his intention to clear the JAM from Basra at 48 hours' notice, redefining the militia and Iranian-supported 'special groups' as insurgents. The resulting *Operation Charge of the Knights* succeeded with US and UK support, but early difficulties damaged Britain's military and political reputation with the US. The UK's credibility with Maliki was also badly damaged, reducing its influence in Baghdad.[11]

At the same time, JAM forces in Sadr City rained rocket fire down on the Iraqi government and international forces in Baghdad's Green Zone. Maliki authorised US and Iraqi forces to clear the area. By concentrating ground troops, armoured vehicles, attack helicopters and armed unmanned aerial vehicles, as well as deploying Iraqi Army units, the Coalition restored security in Sadr City.[12]

The Sunni awakening and the US surge had created the security and political conditions for Maliki to take on Shia extremists and their militias. *Operation Charge of the Knights* was decisive. If it had failed, it would have been difficult to see how both Maliki and the US–UK strategy could have survived.

Iraq assumes security leadership

Once Baghdad was relatively secure, US forces shifted their attention to towns near the capital, which they referred to as the 'Baghdad belts'. There was heavy fighting in these locations, but by 2009 Iraqi forces were holding the areas cleared during the surge, large numbers of Sunni insurgents had switched sides and al-Qaeda was reeling from precision attacks on its leaders and networks by US and Iraqi SOF. The US had shaped the ISF into an effective COIN force that commanded a degree of national respect.

By July 2009, US troops had withdrawn from Iraqi cities. *Operation Iraqi Freedom* was replaced with a 'train, advise and assist' mission. The US negotiated for a Strategic Framework Agreement and a Status of Forces Agreement (SOFA) to cover a longer-term military-assistance mission. But, after the negotiations failed, all US troops were withdrawn from Iraq by mid-December 2011.

In the three years that followed, Maliki consolidated his power.[13] He did so through the persecution of Sunni and Kurd politicians, as well as a toxic combination of discrimination, deliberate neglect and heavy-handed repression of the Sunni minority. Tried and tested police and army commanders were replaced with less capable, politically loyal proxies. This process combined with endemic corruption to greatly reduce the effectiveness of the security forces.

At the same time, the remnants of al-Qaeda in Iraq exploited the recent onset of civil war in Syria. Rebranding itself as the Islamic State, also known as ISIS or ISIL, the group carved out territory centred on its self-proclaimed capital of Raqqa. It rebuilt its networks in Iraqi Sunni communities, carrying out bombings, assassinations and guerrilla attacks on Iraqi security forces. In early 2014, ISIS seized Falluja. In the following months, it gained an increasing advantage over Iraqi government forces stationed near Mosul. Senior Iraqi commanders' decision to flee the city seemed to trigger a rout of their forces, resulting in the disintegration of about one-third of the Iraqi Army. A US-led international coalition intervened to attack ISIS.[14]

Armed politics and the battle of the narrative

The wars in Afghanistan and Iraq can be seen to have validated the principles of US COIN doctrine. High-intensity combat was often essential to clearing key populated areas of insurgents, holding them against insurgent counter-attacks and degrading insurgent networks. It was just as essential to address the root causes of the insurgency by making progress across all areas of governance and development. These latter activities are primarily political. In Iraq, as in most wars, the opposing parties sought not only to cause physical damage to one another, but also to change the perceptions, attitudes and behaviour of their opponents, supporters and third parties.

Both wars saw extensive competition of narratives and ideas in a wide variety of information environments. These included newspapers, radio, terrestrial and satellite television, and cyberspace, particularly social media. As the wars progressed, Coalition, US and NATO operations were increasingly designed in parallel with efforts to influence the attitudes of the enemy, indigenous populations and domestic media. This was accompanied by the growing use of public-opinion polling. When conducted by Afghan civilian companies, polling could reveal attitudes and opinions that Afghans would not easily share with international troops. But for most of the wars in Afghanistan and Iraq, the advantage lay with the insurgents. International forces found it very difficult to conduct success-ful information operations.[15] In the later phases of the wars, social media and smartphones began penetrating the civilian sector. Insurgents generally adapted to these new media faster than the Coalition or ISAF, although by 2013 ISAF was actively monitoring social-media traffic in Afghanistan.[16]

Summarising the role of the political component of COIN in Iraq and Afghanistan, McMaster argued:

> Because an insurgency is fundamentally a political problem, the foundation for detailed counterinsur-gency planning must be a political strategy that drives all other initiatives, actions, and programs. The general objective of the political strategy is to remove

or reduce significantly the political basis for violence. The strategy must be consistent with the nature of the conflict, and is likely to address fears, grievances, and interests that motivate organizations within communities to provide active or tacit support for insurgents. Ultimately, the political strategy must endeavour to convince leaders of reconcilable armed groups that they can best protect and advance their interests through political participation, rather than violence. The political strategy must also foster and maintain a high degree of unity of effort between the supported government and the foreign forces and civilian authorities supporting them.[17]

The Coalition campaign in Iraq was intimately linked to Iraqi politics, and the changing nature of Shia and Sunni politics greatly influenced the war. All the commanders of MNF–I were required to work with the US ambassador to influence the Iraqi government and attempt to harmonise its actions with US political strategy. Some Coalition political action was successful, such as the initiative to support Maliki's confrontation with Shia militias and extremists in 2008. At other times it failed, as seen in the effort to persuade Maliki to sign the SOFA and authorise a follow-on US advice and assistance mission.

In Baghdad and Kabul, the theatre commander and the US ambassador implemented a political strategy. They also had political roles in Washington. A decisive point in this process was the September 2007 congressional testimony by Petraeus and Ambassador Ryan Crocker. By providing credible evidence that the surge in Iraq was having some operational and tactical success, they reduced opposition in Congress and created sufficient political breathing space for the surge to continue into 2008.

Coalition operations and resulting Iraqi perceptions of success could influence Iraqi politics both positively and negatively. For example, an October 2007 US SOF raid in Sadr City unexpectedly resulted in heavy casualties among both Shia militias and Iraqi civilians, causing a political crisis in Baghdad. This prompted widespread criticism of the US from Maliki and other Iraqi politicians, as well as temporary suspension of negotiations over a long-term US–Iraq security agreement. In contrast, the 2008 successes of *Operation Charge of the Knights* and the US clearance of Sadr City reinforced the authority of the Iraqi government, as well as the confidence and standing of Iraqi forces, while greatly reducing the credibility of violent Shia extremists.

The Iraqi authorities occasionally gave prior consent for an operation, only to later repudiate its outcome. This was the case on 25 December 2006, when, as part of an effort to counter infiltration of the Iraqi police by Shia extremists and death squads, British forces in Basra destroyed the extremist base within the notorious Jameat police station. In 2007 Maliki vetoed an initially successful US operation to interdict Shia death squads operating from Sadr City. It is likely that the success of these operations would have threatened the government's political support.

It appears that few Coalition military plans began from the viewpoint of Iraqis or considered outcomes from their perspective. Some British commanders observed that operations were more likely to succeed when they worked with the political forces in Iraqi society, not against them, and that operations were more likely to fail or be rejected by the Iraqis when the Coalition imposed solutions on them.[18]

Operations in southern Afghanistan also reflected the interdependence of war and politics at the tactical level. They have been described and analysed in books by at least three participants in the conflict there. Firstly, the former commander of the British 52nd Infantry Brigade has used this and other examples to develop the concept of 'behavioural conflict'.[19] Secondly, Emile Simpson, a former British officer, has analysed his experiences in Afghanistan in conducting tactical operations where

> the mission, which I experienced as an infantry officer in southern Afghanistan, became indistinguishable from local politics. Given the need to tackle all the problems that stoked insurgency – poor governance, corruption, land rights, ethnic prejudice – it could not have been anything less.[20]

Finally, Carter Malkasian, a US State Department official, has provided a detailed account of the relationship between war and politics in a single district of Afghanistan in *War Comes to Garmser*.[21]

Malkasian shows how, after the fall of the Taliban, Garmser's various tribal groupings achieved a working accommodation under a loose form of governance that balanced their competing interests and antagonisms. But, at the end of 2004, a popular district governor was replaced with a less capable official who was unable to sustain the balance between the tribes. Combined with predatory behaviour by Afghan police and increasing Taliban attacks, this meant that a growing number of tribal elders and local people switched allegiance to the Taliban. By mid-2006, the Taliban had evicted the few remaining pro-government tribal militias, soldiers and police officers, as well as all of the Afghan government presence, apart from a small outpost of British and Afghan troops in the district centre.

Garmser remained largely under Taliban control until mid-2008, when an offensive by the US marines recaptured key territory from the group. British and Afghan troops success-fully held the area, but this still left much of the district under Taliban occupation. The area under Afghan government control was the target of UK-funded development projects, mediated by a community council that sought to involve tribal elders and local stakeholders.

After the US marines deployed reinforcements to Helmand, there was a sustained operation to extend Afghan government control across the rest of the district. Offensive operations cleared Taliban fighters out of key areas, which were then held by combat outposts of marines and Afghan forces. But local politics was just as important. For example, each offen-sive operation accompanied an effort to find a tribal elder with political influence in the relevant area, before paying a limited

Pointers to future conflict: armed politics, counter-insurgency and the battle for the narrative

- Political strategies must include host-nation governments at national, regional and local levels as indepen-dent actors.
- Political strategies must assess the risk that a host-nation government might act in ways that make it part of the prob-lem; this risk can arise from corruption, politicisation and parallel structures.
- Dealing with host-nation govern-ments is likely to require a 'carrot and stick' approach.
- A modern, inter-agency counter-insurgency approach, informed by and influencing politics down to the tactical level, is essential.
- Armed forces would take consid-erable military and political risk in removing counter-insurgency and COIN as core capabilities, as the US and British armies did before 9/11.

- Operations by both conventional state military forces and non-state actors will increasingly feature the 'propaganda of the deed' for this pur-pose.
- It will be as important to be able to manoeuvre in the modern informa-tion environment as in the ground, sea or air domains. Achieving influ-ence is likely to be an increasingly important part of operations – in some cases, as much or more than destroying enemies or securing ter-rain.
- Western forces will need to field information-operations capabilities that are more effective than those deployed in Iraq and Afghanistan. Information operations will need to be seen as central to military plans and their implementation.

number of tribal militiamen to protect that elder and funding quick-impact development projects to reinforce the authority of the Afghan government, district governors and local elders. Over the course of a year, this resulted in the near-complete eviction of the Taliban from the district. In COIN terms, these operations demonstrated the effectiveness of the 'clear, hold, build' approach through a combination of security, local political and development measures.

The three accounts cover different aspects of the conflict between NATO and the Taliban in southern Afghanistan. They convincingly explain the interactions between NATO forces, Afghan forces, warlords, government officials and members of the Taliban. These interactions were influenced by local politics and sought to create local political effects. Force was used as a tool, as were patronage and NATO nations' money.

Conclusion

The wars in Iraq and Afghanistan were originally characterised by high-technology air–land offensive campaigns that caused rapid regime collapse. These campaigns were followed by declarations that major combat operations had ended. Initial hopes of political and security progress disintegrated as the conflicts assumed the character of prolonged, complex and bloody insurgencies. The US and its allies came very close to defeat. In both wars, this outcome was averted by surging troops to conduct counter-insurgency operations – which led to some security improvements – and by transferring responsibility for security leadership to the government in Baghdad or Kabul. After these transitions, security deteriorated.

In the conflicts, fighting was intimately linked with politics at all levels. Domestic politics in Coalition capitals greatly influenced the operations of national contingents. Military operations often had a political impact. And local, national and international politics influenced the course of the wars, both positively and negatively. International forces, insurgents and militias increasingly conducted military operations to create political effects.

CHAPTER TWO

Direction of operations

If strategy is the national alignment of ends, ways and means to achieve strategic objectives, the United States failed to achieve this in the first half of both the Iraq and Afghanistan wars. The conflicts showed that strategy and strategic leadership matter, as does military command at all levels. The challenges of strategic leadership and military command in Iraq and Afghanistan were compounded by the growing unpopularity of the conflicts. This chapter considers the formulation and execution of strategy, military command, coalition and alliance command, and the comprehensive approach.[1] The US strategy-making process during the two wars has been exhaustively described by journalists and in the memoirs of key leaders. The formulation and execution of UK strategy for Iraq between 2001 and 2009 has been thoroughly analysed by the independent Iraq Inquiry, which had complete access to all relevant government documents.[2]

Maximising the chances of success at the strategic, operational and tactical levels requires the integration of all levers of national power. Stabilising Iraq and Afghanistan at every level – from districts through to provinces – required the fullest possible integration of military operations with development and diplomacy. Both wars suggest that, unless military action is part of a comprehensive strategy that leverages the other agencies of government at all relevant levels, its chances of success are greatly reduced. Just as armies use combined-arms tactics to produce a synergy in which the whole is greater than the sum of the parts, a comprehensive approach that fully integrates armed forces, development agencies and diplomacy has the potential to be a similar multiplying factor for the effective implementation of national strategy.

On a number of occasions over the course of the wars, lack of clarity in the alignment of responsibility, authority and accountability created tactical, operational and strategic problems. For example, the role of the United Kingdom in the Coalition Provisional Authority was never clarified by any strategic US–UK agreement. This meant that the UK's influence was essentially informal, a situation that was, according to the Iraq Inquiry, 'a serious weakness which should have been assessed at an early stage'.[3] At the operational level, in Afghanistan in 2006, the UK national command-and-control arrangements were both complex and dysfunctional. Only after major friction between the UK task force in Helmand, the national contingent commander in Kabul, US forces and the NATO chain of command were these arrangements eventually rationalised. And between 2001 and 2010, the US military commander in Afghanistan did not have full authority over all US forces in the country, a source of both frustration and friction.

These problems could also apply at the tactical level. For example, a successful Taliban attack on the joint UK–US base in Helmand in September 2012 resulted in the dismissal of two US Marine Corps generals, who were held accountable for the security breach. The UK chain of command and responsibility for its role in the security of the base was so complex, and accountability and responsibility so diffuse, that no UK officer was held accountable.[4]

A lack of internal clarity also hampered the UK Ministry of Defence (MoD). For example, between 2003 and mid-2006, it was unclear who in the MoD, UK armed forces or their Joint HQ was responsible for formulating the requirements for additional or improved equipment for British forces in Iraq and Afghanistan. This greatly hampered the British response to the threat from improvised explosive devices (IEDs), while creating operational limitations in information, surveillance, target acquisition and reconnaissance (ISTAR), as well as helicopter capability. It was only public, media and political pressure that forced the MoD to streamline its diffuse bureaucracy and align responsibility, authority and accountability, thereby reducing friction and streamlining and accelerating both decision-making and implementation.[5]

Formulation and execution of strategy

The wars in Iraq and Afghanistan show that ensuring responsibility and accountability within the government are aligned as clearly as possible, and that coordination and monitoring arrangements are both clear and simple, are core functions of heads of government and their subordinate teams. So too are strategic decision-making and directing the implementation of these decisions.

The US determined allied strategy in both wars. Sometimes, the US formulation and execution of strategy worked – as it did in the regime changes in Iraq and Afghanistan, as well as the surges in both countries. But the US failed to prevent the rise of Iraqi insurgents and militias.

There were two major interlinked US strategic failures in Iraq. The first was a failure to adequately plan for post-conflict

stabilisation and to respond to the actual (as opposed to anticipated) conditions after regime change. This need not have been
terminal, if the changed conditions had been recognised and an
adequate response executed quickly enough. In the event, this
first failure created the conditions for another: the failure of
US troops to rapidly impose security in Baghdad, the country's
political centre of gravity. As President George W. Bush put it
in his memoirs:

> In the ten months following the invasion we cut troop
> levels from 192,000 to 102,000. Many of the remain-
> ing troops focussed on training the Iraqi army and
> police, not protecting the Iraqi people. We worried we
> could create resentment by looking like occupiers. We
> believed we could train Iraqi security forces to lead
> the fight. And we thought progress towards a repre-
> sentative democracy ... was the best path to lasting
> security.
>
> While there was logic behind these assumptions,
> the Iraqi people's desire for security trumped their
> aversion to occupation ... By reducing our troop
> presence and focussing on training Iraqis, we inad-
> vertently allowed the insurgency to gain momentum.
> Then al Qaeda fighters flocked to Iraq, seeking a new
> safe haven, which made our mission both more diffi-
> cult and more important.[6]

It appears that the US Embassy and military commander in
Baghdad, US Central Command (CENTCOM), the Pentagon,
the State Department and the president all failed to realise that
the situation in Iraq in May 2003 was so different from that
envisaged in US planning that a strategic reassessment was
required. Such a reassessment might have highlighted the need

for not only considerably more troops, but also a much more effective reconstruction effort.

It is likely that the preconceptions of some US strategic leaders may have made it more difficult for them to see that the situation had fundamentally changed. They probably wanted to avoid the uncomfortable implications of having to sustain a much larger contingent in Iraq than originally intended. It would have been possible to do so, but this would have required a higher degree of national military mobilisation, including increasing the size of the US Army and Marine Corps. After 9/11, the US government increased the capabilities, size and freedom to act of the FBI, the CIA, military drones and special-operations forces (SOF). But it appears that the possibility of increasing the size of US ground forces was never seriously discussed until 2007, when Secretary of Defense Robert Gates raised the possibility.

Why did it take more than three and a half years before the president concluded that the transition strategy was failing? Contemporary reports strongly suggest that the success of the various Iraqi elections gave rise to a sense of progress and guarded optimism in both Iraq and Washington. US leaders in Baghdad, CENTCOM and the Pentagon were probably so committed to executing the transition strategy that they regarded the alternatives as offering no likely benefits.

From many published accounts, including his own memoirs, it is clear that two factors had a decisive influence on Bush. The first was his sense, in summer 2006, that the transition strategy was failing and that the war was being lost. The failure to improve security in Baghdad was probably a tipping point. Secondly, analysts and experts outside the formal US national-security structure convinced him that a surge was a feasible option.[7]

The US also failed to prevent the deterioration of security in Afghanistan between 2004 and 2010, a consequence of the

2002 choice to make Iraq a higher priority than Afghanistan. Benefiting from only finite amounts of political attention and military-planning capacity – as well military intelligence, diplomatic and development resources – it was not until 2009 that the allies had the organisational capacity and strategic bandwidth to give Afghanistan the attention it deserved.

There are many accounts of President Barack Obama's 2009 decision to surge US troops into Afghanistan showing that he used the National Security Council as a vehicle for extended deliberations over US strategy, assessing the multiple factors that affected the war. He scrutinised and challenged the military recommendations for implementing a counter-insurgency strategy and the need for a surge of US troops. He also encouraged Vice President Joe Biden to offer an alternative strategy. This gave Obama the opportunity to deeply understand and scrutinise the strategic situation, test the options available to him and satisfy himself of the military and political logic of the US plan.

The effectiveness of UK strategic leadership also varied during the two wars. In 2001 the UK deployed aircraft, cruise missiles and SOF to join the US attack on the Taliban, and subsequently led the deployment of the International Security Assistance Force (ISAF) to Kabul. In 2003 the UK also deployed a substantial force to take part in the US-led operation to remove the Iraqi regime. This was the UK's only unqualified strategic success in Iraq.

In the Second World War and the Falklands War, prime ministers Winston Churchill and Margaret Thatcher used war cabinets to exercise strategic leadership – for both decision-making and monitoring the implementation of those decisions. It is unclear whether this option was ever considered for Iraq. The evidence presented to the Iraq Inquiry paints a picture of strategic leadership and management of the Iraqi and Afghan wars that fell below the standards achieved by Churchill and Thatcher. Prime Minister Tony Blair had previously displayed an ability to take strategic decisions and see them implemented. His role in the Northern Ireland peace process is a clear example of this. But Iraq was a more difficult strategic challenge, and became even more so as the popularity of the war declined.

The Iraq Inquiry provides overwhelming evidence that Blair's leadership and management of post-conflict stabilisation in Iraq was insufficient. Many of the decision-making structures appear to have been ad hoc. This need not have been a problem, provided that implementation of strategic decisions was properly managed. While there is abundant evidence that decisions were made, there is equally abundant evidence that these decisions either were not followed up or were insufficiently coordinated, and that progress was not adequately monitored.

There is considerable evidence that politicians, government departments and senior officials not only ignored direction given by the prime minister but were allowed to do so. For instance, following a June 2003 visit to Iraq, Blair told ministers that the British government should return to 'a war footing' to avoid 'losing the peace in Iraq'. The Iraq Inquiry concludes that there were 'no indications that Mr Blair's direction led to any substantive changes in the UK's reconstruction effort'.[8]

Reading between the lines, it appears that Nigel Sheinwald, the prime minister's foreign-policy adviser for much of the post-conflict phase of the war, attempted to energise the UK effort in Whitehall, but was unable to overcome bureaucratic inertia and conflicting ministerial and departmental agendas.

The Inquiry suggested that the appointment of a single senior minister to lead the British post-conflict stabilisation and reconstruction of Iraq might have improved strategy formulation and implementation. This presumes the availability of a minister with sufficient leadership skills and a head of government well versed in the implementation of strategy to both identify needs and confer the necessary authority. Alternative options would have been to use the deputy prime minister, cabinet secretary and Blair's chief of staff, all of whom could have used their authority to impose the necessary discipline on government ministries. There is no evidence that Blair considered any of these options.

Having accepted responsibility for the post-conflict occupation of four provinces in southern Iraq, the UK (like the US) was surprised by the extensive looting that followed the collapse of the regime. Although the British government had also been warned about the deterioration of infrastructure in Iraq, it was still alarmed by what it found. It became apparent to British commanders in Basra and officials in London that the situation was significantly different from the one that had been envisaged. The Iraq Inquiry concluded that the significant changes to the situation in Iraq between August 2003 and August 2004 should have prompted a strategic reassessment by London. No such reassessment took place.[9]

The Inquiry concluded that the UK failed to achieve any of its strategic objectives by the time of the British withdrawal from Iraq in 2009. UK planning for post-conflict stabilisation and reconstruction was 'wholly inadequate'. The scale of the UK effort in post-conflict Iraq 'failed to take account of the magnitude of the task of stabilising, administering and reconstructing Iraq, and of the responsibilities which were likely to fall to the UK'. Throughout the war, the UK reconstruction effort in Iraq suffered from poor coordination between government departments in London and inadequate civil–military cooperation in Iraq. There was no coherent UK strategy for security-sector reform. This was because Blair 'did not ensure that there was a flexible, realistic and fully resourced plan that integrated UK military and civilian contributions'.[10] A particularly serious problem was an 'optimism bias' in assessments of the situation, which could be at variance from the actual situation in Iraq.[11]

This corresponds with contemporary assessments made by British military commanders in Basra. They sensed a profound lack of civil–military coordination in London, a lack of top-down leadership and a government approach to Iraq that was under-resourced and inadequately led.[12] As General Richard Dannatt, chief of the British Army in 2006–09, put it in 2010, 'we failed to organize ourselves properly in a single, transparent chain of authority, with the result that internecine squabbling over roles, resources and responsibilities dangerously damaged the combined effect we were trying to achieve'.[13]

This is only one of a large number of examples of sub-optimal performance by politicians, government departments, intelligence staff, senior military officers and civilian officials. For example, pre-invasion planning in Whitehall had noted that post-conflict operations would be decisive; a major reconstruction effort would be necessary; US plans for post-conflict activity were weak; and the rapidly improvised Office for Reconstruction and Humanitarian Assistance (ORHA) would be overwhelmed by the task. But no one person or department was placed in charge of pre-war planning for reconstruction. Development minister Clare Short displayed 'reluctance to engage in post-conflict activity other than for the immediate humanitarian response to conflict, until it was confirmed that the UN would lead the reconstruction effort'.[14] Leadership of the UK reconstruction effort was eventually given to the Foreign and Commonwealth Office (FCO) in late March 2003. Although an ad hoc committee considered reconstruction plans, it assumed no effective role in implementation.

Despite an agreement between Short and Foreign Secretary Jack Straw that the UK should do more to support the ORHA, the Department for International Development (DfID) effectively opted out of the task. After Short's resignation in May 2003, DfID assumed leadership of reconstruction, but by then the UK effort had fallen well behind the requirements – and well behind Blair's public and private rhetoric. Relations between DfID and the British military were badly damaged, and took years to recover.

There were also strategic failures by the FCO. For instance, at a July 2003 cabinet meeting, Blair concluded that the UK should make the Coalition Provisional Authority (CPA) regional office in Basra, or CPA (South), 'a model'. In a subsequent video conference, Blair told Bush and other US strategic leaders that the UK would do its 'level best to meet any demand for additional resources'.[15] A senior diplomat, Hilary Synnott, was called out of retirement to head the team.

The Iraq Inquiry identified abundant evidence that the UK never provided the requested staff or resources. The FCO's permanent under-secretary failed to ensure that the department provided 'adequate practical support to Sir Hilary Synnott as Head of CPA (South)'. The Inquiry did not explain why the inadequate implementation of a cabinet decision, which had been declared to the US government, was tolerated by the central coordinating machinery of government, the foreign secretary or the prime minister.

In his memoirs, Synnott claims that the consistent failure of the FCO to provide sufficient personnel

> stemmed from a lack of political direction. Seen from Iraq and notwithstanding Blair's rhetoric, there was little evidence that the British Government as a whole saw itself as being at war. Management and oversight

at ministerial and senior official level was essentially ad hoc and bore little resemblance to the highly organised arrangements for post-conflict reconstruction which had been put in place, for instance, some four years before the end of the Second World War. Blair put a constant public emphasis on the importance and urgency of making progress in Iraq. But, seemingly little interested in the processes within Government by which this might be brought about, he proved unable to mobilise Government departments to produce the necessary results.[16]

The persistent weakness of UK strategic leadership between 2001 and 2009 shows that, while decision-making by strategic leaders is important, implementing their decisions is just as important. This entails efforts to make sure that decisions are converted into plans that assign roles to those responsible for implementation. Implementation then needs to be monitored to assess whether it is succeeding, and whether the situation has changed enough to require that the plan either be adjusted or replaced.

Successful strategic leaders ensure that plans are implemented. As well as relying on the existing strategic coordinating machinery, they check implementation for themselves, not only through constant communication with their principal staff, but also by visiting the front-line. They can also make use of 'directed telescopes', such as personal representatives empowered to provide unvarnished assessments of the 'ground truth', as well as the degree to which subordinate organisations are implementing the strategy and providing accurate assessments. There is nothing new about these approaches. Successful strategic leaders in the military, business and politics have consistently employed them. But the Iraq Inquiry suggests that Blair did not use them as part of his leadership approach in the Iraq and Afghan wars.

In autumn 2009, Prime Minister Gordon Brown improved strategic management of British operations in Afghanistan by setting up a specific committee for this purpose. This followed a summer of significant casualties and growing controversy over the size, equipment and resources available to British troops in Helmand. Brown's initiative improved the coherence of British efforts in Afghanistan

Prime Minister David Cameron chaired a meeting of a new National Security Council on his first day in office, in May 2010. The council became the principal forum for the formulation of British defence, intelligence and security strategy, and for monitoring the execution of that strategy in Afghanistan and Libya, and against the Islamic State, also known as ISIS or ISIL. While the new body was imperfect, many UK military and security officials regarded it as having significantly improved the formulation and execution of strategy.[17]

Pointers to future conflict: formulation and execution of strategy

- Strategic leaders need to ensure that decisions are converted into plans that assign roles to those responsible for implementation. Implementation needs to be monitored to assess whether it is succeeding or requires either adjustments to the plan or the formulation of a new one.
- Strategic leaders must ensure that responsibility and accountability within government is as clear as possible and that coordination and monitoring arrangements are both clear and simple.
- Strategic leaders must check imple- mentation for themselves through constant communication with their principal staff, visits to the front-line and personal representatives empowered to provide unvarnished assessments.
- During a war, the character of the conflict and the utility of force must be regularly re-assessed at every level, from the tactical to the strategic.
- Assumptions made by senior leaders may need regular challenge and validation – not least to identify self-imposed limitations that constrain military and political options.

The strengths and weaknesses of US and UK strategy formulation and execution suggest that, during a war, the character of the conflict and the utility of force must be regularly reassessed at every level, from the tactical to the strategic. The national strategic decision-making machinery must regularly and objectively assess whether the implementation of strategy is on track. Assumptions made by senior leaders may need to be repeatedly challenged and validated, not least to identify self-imposed limitations on military and political options. 'Group think' also needs to be challenged, in part by actively seeking alternative assessments from outside experts.

Military command

Military command is the authority to order and direct the implementation of decisions made by the commander. Military doctrine emphasises the principle of 'unity of command'. This makes military commanders at every level the single point of responsibility and accountability for the actions of formations and units allocated to them.

Military command could not be applied to civilian and international agencies, let alone the host nation. Military commanders in Iraq and Afghanistan instead attempted to achieve 'unity of effort', realising common objectives through cooperation rather than command. This depended on personal interaction. For example, in 2004, Lieutenant-General Ricardo Sanchez (commander of Combined Joint Task Force 7, or CJTF-7) and Ambassador Paul Bremer (head of the CPA) had a sub-optimal working relationship. In contrast, in 2007, General David Petraeus and Ambassador Ryan Crocker set out to promote cooperation between the Multi-National Force–Iraq (MNF-I) and the US Embassy.

The wars showed the value of a hierarchy of headquarters with clearly defined roles, as well as the key role played by the theatre HQ and commander, who needed well-developed judgement, interpersonal skills and the ability to communicate military matters to a wide variety of non-military actors. The experience of Iraq and Afghanistan also highlights the need for commanders to have an effective headquarters in which they have complete confidence – not least in its ability to manage and control its role in the war on a day-to-day basis.

The more complicated and uncertain the command-and-control relationship, the more energy military commanders have to expend working around its complexities and lack of clarity. A significant problem in Afghanistan was achieving unity of command, not only between US and NATO forces, but also within US forces. It was only in 2010 that all US troops in the country were finally placed under unified command.[18]

In both Iraq and Afghanistan, US generals served as the theatre commanders throughout the wars – with the exception of May 2006–February 2007, when ISAF HQ was based in a British-led multinational headquarters. Although these US commanders were subordinated to CENTCOM, they dealt directly with Washington – the chairman of the Joint Chiefs of Staff, the secretary of defence and the president – on key issues. The political sensitivity of both wars meant that it was essential that these three leaders had complete confidence in their theatre commanders.

At times, this confidence waned. The first occasion was in autumn and winter 2006, as Bush lost confidence in the Iraq transition strategy. When the strategy changed to the surge, the president decided that a new theatre commander and a new US ambassador would be needed to execute it. Petraeus and Crocker were selected for these roles. Similarly, in June 2009, Gates and Chairman of the Joint Chiefs of Staff Admiral Michael Mullen decided to replace ISAF commander General David McKiernan with General Stanley McChrystal. But the leaking of McChrystal's assessment of the campaign to the media undermined some of the confidence that Obama had in him. After *Rolling Stone* magazine published an article in which some of McChrystal's staff criticised the president, the general was dismissed.

Command at the theatre and operational levels

The US military characterised the highest headquarters in Iraq and Afghanistan as 'theatre-strategic': much of their role – liaison with the host government, the US Embassy, the CIA, key allies and international organisations – required operating at the highest political and military levels. This level of command was represented by MNF–I HQ, the various high-level headquarters in Afghanistan and then by ISAF HQ.

There were also many lower-level military functions, such as coordinating the tactical actions of subordinate divisions. In theory, all the functions could be combined into a single headquarters. After regime change in Iraq, command of Coalition forces passed to an ad hoc headquarters based on US Army 7 Corps HQ, commanded by the newly promoted Lieutenant-General Sanchez. This tactical HQ had not prepared for its theatre-level role as CJTF-7 and the high-level civil–military responsibilities that this entailed. It never received more than a small fraction of the staff it required for its new function.

Unsurprisingly, this ill-supported and unprepared headquarters was overwhelmed. These inadequate military arrangements were complemented by considerable civil–military friction. Relations between Sanchez and Bremer were poor. The CPA itself had far too few high-quality staff and its understandable focus on Baghdad meant that it contributed little to reconstruction efforts outside the capital.

From mid-2004 onwards, the overstretched US military headquarters was expanded into MNF–I HQ as the overall theatre headquarters, commanded by General George Casey. It had two subordinate headquarters: Multinational Corps–Iraq, acting as a land-component headquarters at corps level, which planned, led and coordinated land tactical operations; and Multinational Security Transition Command–Iraq, responsible for Iraqi military and police capacity-building. These arrangements greatly improved the effectiveness of military command and control. The model was also applied for much, but not all, of the war in Afghanistan. It was important to separate the high-level political–military headquarters from the headquarters executing the land campaign. It is likely that the US will apply this model to similar operations in future.

Common pointers to theatre and operational command emerge from the memoirs of several US and UK theatre commanders, as well as from other open-source material.[19] The first is the need for the commander to think and act at the relevant level. Tactical operations were often complex and politically sensitive, especially when there were heavy casualties. But a higher commander who thought and acted primarily at the tactical level would not have the time, energy or capacity to act at the operational or strategic level.

Secondly, the commander needs to understand the political situation and be able to interact with national, allied and host-nation political leaders. This requires not only a good understanding of the political dimension of the war, but also a high level of empathy and other interpersonal skills, together with a large amount of patience. The commander will be working alongside ambassadors from troop-contributing nations, who will want to lead on many political issues. The commander of an international force will inevitably become as much a political actor as a military one.

Heads of government, defence ministers and chiefs of defence all need to have confidence in the commanders of their national contingents. This must be established from the outset of their command, if not before, as any major incident or significant casualties will test the relationship – possibly to destruction. Chiefs of defence staff often play a key role in establishing such confidence.

Command at the tactical level
Divisional headquarters integrated the efforts of indigenous forces, civilian agencies and host-nation local authorities to give tactical direction and coordination to brigades. US divisions controlled considerable divisional assets, particularly integral US Army aviation, which they allocated to subordinate brigades to reflect the division's priorities. This allowed them to designate a main effort and allocate resources to support it. The US Army and many other NATO armies concluded that the wars in Iraq and Afghanistan reinforced the need for the conventional Western hierarchy of headquarters from platoon to corps. They feel the divisional level of command has proved its value as the tactical gearing between brigade and corps level.

Most of the armies that took part in these wars were structured to allow their deployable formations and units to manoeuvre, requiring headquarters that were capable of changing location as battles ebbed and flowed. But, for stabilisation operations, headquarters were deployed to fixed bases. This increased their effectiveness by allowing commanders and staff to work in less austere conditions, and by enabling them to use high-capacity communications. Both wars also saw the routine allocation to divisions and brigades of capabilities formerly held at corps and higher levels. These include air–land integration, ISTAR assets previously held at high levels and military reconstruction teams. This change increased the capability of these formations, but increased the size of the headquarters.

Pointers to future conflict: military command

- There should be a hierarchy of headquarters with clearly defined roles, besides the key role played by the theatre headquarters and commander.
- High-level commanders must have well-developed judgement, interpersonal skills and the ability to communicate military matters to a wide variety of non-military actors.
- Commanders must have effective headquarters in which they have complete confidence, not least in their ability to manage and control their roles in the war on a day-to-day basis.
- The ability to connect headquarters and units to high-capacity secure bandwidth will be invaluable, but against a more capable enemy, large static headquarters will be extremely vulnerable.

These trends meant that formation headquarters became increasingly fixed. But unit headquarters remained smaller, less elaborate organisations. Although these headquarters were usually located in fixed bases, offensive operations to clear insurgents required battalion commanders and their staff to deploy to the field. Tactical commanders needed to be able to visit their subordinate units to assess the situation, adjust plans and sustain the morale of troops. They required the ability to move across the battlefield using a variety of means, including helicopters and armoured vehicles.[20]

International forces' command of the electromagnetic spectrum remained largely undisputed in both wars. Although headquarters were sometimes targeted in rocket attacks, none of them resulted in significant disruption. The ability to provide headquarters and units with access to high-capacity, secure bandwidth will be invaluable in the future, but large static headquarters would be extremely vulnerable against a more capable enemy.

Coalition and alliance command

The experience of Iraq and Afghanistan suggests that, in operations in which its forces predominate, the US will effectively lead the formulation and execution of strategy, so NATO can probably play only a supporting role. Nevertheless, the ISAF experience shows how NATO can improve a multinational operation. The Alliance does so by providing legitimacy, helping to generate forces and supplying a structured high-level political–military forum that can assist with managing the operation. It can also provide a force-generation mechanism, as well as techniques and procedures that promote inter-operability. Peacetime military engagement with other nations' armed forces – through multinational exercises and, where necessary, capacity-building – will make it easy to assemble future multinational forces. The ability to lead multinational forces will remain an enduring requirement for senior commanders.

The memoirs of key US actors portray NATO as principally a means for securing additional troops for Afghanistan. But the organisation had much wider political value as a strategic political–military forum in which the US could consult its allies. This provided political legitimacy for some member states, as well as the non-NATO states that joined ISAF as 'partners'. NATO summits became venues in which the Alliance reaffirmed its political and military commitment to Afghanistan, often by announcing major strategic milestones and initiatives.

The wars reaffirmed the well-tested principles for commanding a multinational force: commanders and staffs needed to understand different national contingents' capabilities and limitations; demonstrate mutual respect, tolerance and patience; and allow for the extra time required to orchestrate multinational operations. The top commanders in Baghdad and Kabul found that this activity (including hosting visits by politicians and senior defence officials from national contingents) occupied much of their time.

The US might have been able to conduct both wars without the aid of other countries, but this would have increased the already considerable demands on US forces. The involvement of other nations in the campaigns demonstrated international commitment to both operations, but created military and political friction and risks, especially for the commanders of multinational forces.

Some nations brought capabilities that complemented those of the US. For example, the Italian Carabinieri had a unique set of paramilitary policing skills that were put to good use in training the Iraqi and Afghan police. British officers played an instrumental role in leading efforts to reconcile with Sunni insurgents in Iraq. The UK also entered the war with more highly developed counter-IED capabilities than the rest of the Coalition, including the US. The transfer of these skills allowed the US and other nations to rapidly improve their own capabilities.

But many nations had a less developed military capability than the US. For instance, British forces had far fewer unmanned aerial vehicles than US troops. Many contingents had far fewer precision weapons and less helicopter support than US forces. As time went on, the US increasingly assigned its own forces to reduce these capability gaps – for example, providing US Air Force casualty-evacuation helicopters to UK, Canadian and Dutch forces in southern Afghanistan. The US provided more than 1,000 mine-resistant ambush-protected vehicles to allies in Afghanistan.

Air forces from different nations faced comparatively few challenges in operating together. Common use of English was a factor, as was the comparative ease with which they could integrate their efforts into the CENTCOM air component. Widespread adoption of NATO techniques and procedures provided a form of military lubrication, making it easier for the forces of NATO allies and partners to operate together.

Both campaigns showed that there were considerable practical challenges in combined operations between land forces of different nations. The largest of these challenges was the limited ability of the command-and-control systems of most nations to exchange messages and data. This reduced situational awareness and increased the risk of 'blue-on-blue' (friendly-fire) incidents. Attempts to overcome this included the traditional practice of exchanging liaison teams and the transfer of the US Blue Force Tracker system to its allies. In Afghanistan from 2010 onwards, NATO established a common mission network that extended from ISAF HQ to all national contingents.

Different national approaches and the 'patchwork effect'
As conditions in different parts of Iraq and Afghanistan varied, the campaign plan was interpreted differently from province to province. But the approaches employed on the ground by national contingents varied even more, reflecting different military experience, cultures, organisations, tactics and training. There were also differing strategic reasons for committing troops. Some parties, such as the UK, sought to sustain their military–strategic relationship with the US. Others, such as Georgia, contributed troops to ISAF to strengthen their chances of being admitted to NATO. National law was also an important factor: constitutional limitations meant that the role of the Japanese contingent in Iraq was limited to reconstruction and development. Their policy on the use of force was so restrictive that they had to be protected by Australian troops.

Few nations were prepared to take as much risk or endure as many casualties as the US. For instance, the March 2004 Madrid bombings led to the withdrawal of the Spanish contingent from Iraq. During the spring 2004 Shia uprisings in Iraq, Kiev placed the Ukrainian Brigade under restrictions that prevented it from doing much more than defend its camp. As a result, the CPA withdrew from Kut. It was only after US troops were assigned to the area that the militias were defeated and the CPA office restored. At the same time, the British battalion in Amarah did everything it could to defend the CPA office there.[21] The deaths of ten French soldiers in an ambush in Afghanistan in August 2008 prompted Paris to order an immediate reduction in operational activity, which was followed by the withdrawal of the French contingent earlier than planned.

In Afghanistan, nations took differing approaches to reconstruction and development in general, and to the role and employment of Provincial Reconstruction Teams (PRTs) in particular. They interpreted ISAF rules of engagement, including measures to counter suicide bombers or riots, in different ways. Countries also had differing policies for investigating complaints made by civilians, and for compensating civilians for damage, injury or death resulting from military operations. This was another source of friction.

All these factors meant that most countries placed specific limits on the actions of their contingents, the so-called 'national caveats'. One exception was the Estonian contingent in ISAF, as Tallinn sought to maximise its influence in NATO by imposing no national caveats at all. By and large, the US was able to work around such caveats in Iraq, but in 2009 they became a serious military and political issue in Afghanistan. McChrystal, and later Petraeus, sought the support of NATO to reduce the number of caveats, with limited success.

An important consequence of these factors was that there was considerable variation between national contingents' execution of campaign and tactical plans. This was sometimes described as creating a 'patchwork effect'. The conscious choice not to change the UK's transition strategy in Basra after 2006 to match the US surge almost resulted in strategic defeat. This illustrates how using a different strategy, operational design or tactical approach to the rest of a coalition land component creates the risk of tactical incoherence. One measure employed

Pointers to future conflict: coalition and alliance command

- In operations in which US forces predominate, the US will effectively lead the formulation and execution of strategy.
- NATO can improve a multinational operation by providing legitimacy, helping to generate forces, promoting inter-operability and providing a structured high-level political–military forum that can assist with managing operations.
- Peacetime military engagement with other nations' armed forces, including both multinational exercises and capacity-building, will make it easy to assemble future multinational forces.
- The ability to lead multinational forces will remain an enduring requirement for senior commanders. Commanders and their staff need to understand the capabilities and limitations of different national contingents; demonstrate mutual respect, tolerance and patience; and allow extra time for the orchestration of multinational operations.

by the US to reduce this friction and inconsistency was training and mentoring national contingents. For example, US Marine mentors were deployed with the Georgian contingent in Helmand.

Reconstruction and the comprehensive approach

Before 9/11, the US and many of its allies had considerable experience providing reconstruction and development assistance overseas. This was usually the lead activity of an international-development organisation such as the US Agency for International Development or the UK's DfID.

In NATO operations in Bosnia and Kosovo, the security situation had for the most part been sufficiently benign that development agencies required little military assistance. The Office of the High Representative for Bosnia and Herzegovina and the UN mission in Kosovo were both able to coordinate reconstruction and development, and to play key political roles. In contrast, US and NATO forces did not play a leading role in reconstruction.[22]

In both Iraq and Afghanistan, many Coalition states declared that a comprehensive approach was essential. This means, in

NATO's definition, that 'political, civilian and military instruments need to be involved in the planning and conduct of operations'.[23] In much more challenging circumstances than in the Balkans, the US and many of its allies struggled to adequately integrate their military operations with the rest of their strategic tools, particularly diplomacy and development. It was particularly difficult to achieve the necessary levels of civilian support and unity of effort.

All the evidence suggests that the US failed to adequately plan for the non-military aspects of the occupation of Iraq. Before 9/11, there had been very little joint training between diplomats, development professionals and the military; the problems this created were exacerbated by legal restrictions on the movement of money between US government departments. In many parts of Iraq, the lack of effective civilian organisation, expertise or financial assistance forced additional responsibilities onto the shoulders of military officers, who were often operating well beyond their training and experience.

The memoirs of senior US officers – as well as those of Gates and his predecessor, Donald Rumsfeld – are full of expressions of frustration at the State Department's inability to deploy the required number of civilian staff. Those deployed were often too junior and served for too short a time to understand the situation well enough to make a difference. A Pentagon assessment concluded that:

> Initially in Iraq and Afghanistan, interagency unity of effort was a resounding failure. DOD partnering with other US departments and agencies during the first half of the decade consistently failed to harness the strengths and resources of the respective organizations ... The biggest lesson for the US from the first five years of war in Iraq was 'the inability to apply and

focus the full resources and capabilities of the US in a concerted and coherent way'. Despite the criticality of unity of effort among elements of the US government for these operations, it was slow to develop and was largely personality-dependent. In fact, in Iraq, the notable unity of effort that was finally achieved was largely because of deliberate efforts of both military and civilian leaders.[24]

For the comprehensive approach to work, organisations with very different institutional cultures had to work together. In most cases, the military had access to a much larger budget and more personnel, particularly planning staff, than other organisations, but often lacked people with the necessary civilian skills. There was no inter-agency doctrine of any substance that could provide common terminology or frames of reference between the organisations in the way that US and NATO joint doctrine helped bind together the different armed services. Success often depended on key individuals who were determined to bridge organisational gaps by working together.

A major challenge in Afghanistan was the constitution and culture of the Afghan government. This made the comprehensive approach much more difficult to implement at the provincial and district levels. According to Malkasian,

> under Afghan law, police chiefs and other district officials were not appointed by the district governor. They were appointed in Kabul by the head of their respective ministry; in the case of a police chief, by the Ministry of the Interior. The district governor was senior to the police chief, but the police chief answered to the provincial police chief. The same was technically true of the provincial governor. He did

not appoint the provincial police chief, NDS (intelligence) director, or other line ministry directors. If
he wanted to make a change, he had to argue with
Kabul. Thus, the district governor was senior in name
only. He had no real power over the police chief, NDS
chief, or line directors. They were supposed to obey
his wishes, but, if they did not, the district governor's
only recourse was to complain to the provincial governor, who would then have to pressure the provincial
police chief or Ministry of Interior, expending his own
political capital along the way.[25]

This made it much more difficult for Afghan officials to apply
the comprehensive approach for themselves. It also meant that
international forces and civilian political and development
officials had to work to understand the personal dynamics
between Afghan officials at the provincial and district levels, to
identify where they could best focus their efforts to influence
Afghan leaders and best direct their money for development
projects.

In general, the better the understanding achieved and the
more the patience displayed, the more likely it is that international efforts to apply the comprehensive approach at the
local level will succeed. There appears to have been greater
unity of effort in Afghan districts controlled by the Taliban
than those controlled by the Coalition, as shown by the fact
that there was far less internal friction between Taliban military commanders and civilian officials, including governors
and judges.

The US was not alone in encountering difficulties and friction in reconstruction and implementing the comprehensive
approach. The UK experience also shows that the execution
of the comprehensive approach depends on national strate-

gic leadership. The Iraq Inquiry concluded that, in 2003, 'the UK failed to plan or prepare for the major reconstruction programme required in Iraq', and 'these failures persisted in the post-conflict period. They included poor inter-departmental co-ordination, inadequate civilian–military co-operation and a failure to use resources coherently.'[26] It was only in early 2009 that a UK government-level inter-agency plan was agreed in London. The delay had created problems in applying the comprehensive approach.[27]

After *Operation Charge of the Knights* in spring 2008, the execution of the comprehensive approach in Basra improved. But its leadership was informal, and depended on the personal chemistry of the British military commander, the head of the UK PRT, the UK consul general and the head of the US Regional Embassy Office. Joint military–civilian assessments, joint planning teams and joint delivery teams all assisted with this integration.

From 2003 onwards, PRTs were created in Afghanistan to further reconstruction and development. They were multi-agency teams of military and civilian personnel, including diplomats and development-agency staff, as well as other experts in fields such as policing, agriculture and justice. Located in provincial capitals, they worked to extend the reach of the Afghan government at the provincial and district levels by using funds from the US and other nations to promote local reconstruction and development.

There was a wide variation in PRT organisation and operations, reflecting not only the local situation in different provinces, but also the considerably different approaches by the nations that provided them. In Afghanistan, PRTs fielded by the US were predominantly staffed by the military, while in Iraq they were generated by the State Department. In the 2006–14 deployment to Helmand Province, the UK set out to maximise the chances of successfully implementing the comprehensive approach. The deputy commander of the UK brigade was also deputy head of the large PRT located in the provincial capital. During most of the British deployment in Helmand, the PRT and the brigade HQ were co-located.

Where the concept worked well, it could bring together development and military efforts, but there was always the risk of emphasising short-term projects, which made the presence of international forces more acceptable, rather than sustainable, longer-term development. Particularly in Afghanistan, PRT efforts could either overwhelm fragile Afghan local-governance capabilities or inadvertently empower malign actors. But, as fighting in Afghanistan intensified, the teams were often the only source of development assistance in contested areas, as non-governmental organisations found it difficult to operate. It is likely that the militaries concerned consider the PRT concept to be only a qualified success, but will consider it relevant to future stabilisation operations.[28]

The comprehensive approach can only be fully effective at the tactical level if there is an integrated inter-agency plan at the national strategic and operational levels that sets the framework for individual departmental planning. This joint approach can be enabled by the co-location of headquarters and staffs, and the mutual embedding of staffs.

The diplomatic services and development agencies of many countries became more capable of operating in the difficult environments of Iraq and Afghanistan as the wars progressed. Keeping the inter-agency approach alive requires leadership and support from politicians and senior officials in the armed forces and relevant government departments. On this basis, concrete plans can be made for joint education and training in peace, and to develop the practical measures to better coop-erate on exercises that provide practical tests of inter-agency cooperation. It should be possible to insist on mandatory inter-agency education for key personnel.

Some countries have declared their intent to retain this capability. For instance, the UK maintains its inter-agency Stabilisation Unit, jointly funded and staffed by the MoD, the FCO and DfID. It is an integrated civil–military unit designed to assist government responses to crises and efforts to build stability. The UK has also created a pool of deployable civilian experts for responding to overseas crises, and promotes inter-agency cooperation through pooled funds, shared between government departments.

There are probably limitations on the ability of civilians to work in high-risk hostile environments. So there is a case for armed forces to retain their own development and reconstruction experts, who will be able to operate where civilians cannot. Once the environment becomes less hostile, they can better coordinate the military and civilian reconstruction and development efforts. The US Army is retaining its Civil Affairs Brigades, partly for this purpose.

Pointers to future conflict: reconstruction and the comprehensive approach

- Unless military action is part of a comprehensive strategy that leverages the other agencies of government at all relevant levels, its chances of success are greatly reduced.
- The comprehensive approach can only be fully effective at the tactical level if there is an integrated inter-agency plan at the national strategic and operational levels. This joint approach can be enabled by co-location of headquarters and staff, as well as by mutually embedding staff.
- Keeping the inter-agency approach alive requires leadership and support from politicians and senior officials in the armed forces and government departments to enable joint education and training in peace, including mandatory inter-agency education for key personnel.
- There is a case for armed forces to retain their own development and reconstruction experts. These experts will be able to operate in hostile environments where civilians cannot, and can co-ordinate military and civilian reconstruction and development efforts in more benign circumstances.

CHAPTER THREE

Military capability, tactics and operations

Although the United States and its allies achieved regime change in Iraq and Afghanistan, the unforeseen demands of stabilisation and counter-insurgency operations meant the character of the conflicts was much more violent than antici-pated. Indeed, many of these operations involved sustained heavy fighting and extensive use of improvised explosive devices (IEDs) by insurgents and militias. Thus, international forces had to make far greater use of combat capabilities than they had in the Balkans. Many of these capabilities underwent considerable adaptation.

In 2001 the Taliban's military equipment was largely obsolete. The few aircraft, air-defence systems and armoured vehicles it had were overmatched by US air-delivered weapons assisted by modern surveillance and command networks. Regime change depended on the ground forces of the Northern Alliance, with US special-operations forces (SOF) acting as the interface between these forces and a mixture of long-range US Air Force (USAF) bombers, US Navy aircraft based on carriers in the Indian Ocean and USAF fighters operating from bases in the Persian Gulf – all of which made extensive use of air-to-air refuelling.

Iraqi forces had many aircraft, air-defence systems and armoured vehicles. But they lacked sufficient training, and their equipment largely dated back to the 1980s and had not been modernised. The US and UK forces that invaded Iraq in 2003 displayed a high degree of air–land synergy; precision attack and rapid manoeuvre by well-equipped and well-trained land and air forces led to the defeat of the Iraqi military more quickly than many commentators had predicted.

At the operational and strategic levels, the speed of the US ground advance outstripped even the worst-case calculations of Iraq's leaders. This, combined with attacks on Iraqi command-and-control and information, surveillance, target-acquisition and reconnaissance (ISTAR) capabilities, meant that Iraqi forces' understanding of the situation slipped so far behind events that they were unable to mount an effective counter-attack. Nonetheless, assaults carried out by irregulars created tactical surprise and strategic shock for US forces. In Afghanistan, the Taliban was initially prepared to mass large numbers of fighters, employing conventional infantry tactics. But in the face of allied attacks using artillery, helicopters and aircraft, these tactics were abandoned in favour of ambushes and the placement of a large number of IEDs, an adaptation that was accelerated by the exploitation of the internet. In 2009–10, the density of IEDs laid in some areas of southern Afghanistan approached that of a conventional minefield.[1]

Irregular forces in both countries made use of the vast amount of unguarded arms and ammunition left over after the fall of the regimes. Common tactics included ambushes with small arms and rocket-propelled grenades; mortar and rocket attacks on security forces' bases; and ambushes of helicopters and low-flying aircraft using a limited number of man-portable air-defence systems.

In Iraq, Shia political parties exploited nationalism, disillusion with the Coalition and unemployment to organise militias. The degrees of confrontation with the Coalition varied but, from 2005 onwards, elements of Jaish al-Mahdi (JAM) sought to gain political influence by attacking Coalition forces. The Islamic Revolutionary Guard Corps's Quds Force covertly aided hard-line Shia 'special groups' in attacks on international forces. Iranian-supplied explosively formed projectile (EFP) bombs greatly increased the effectiveness of these groups.[2]

Sunni insurgents in Iraq and the Taliban in Afghanistan also made effective use of suicide bombers, many of whom drove cars and trucks packed with explosives in mass-casualty attacks. The Taliban employed jihadist volunteers as suicide fighters. These militants usually participated in well-planned and -rehearsed 'spectacular' attacks, in which they seized politically important targets before fighting to the death.

In both countries, insurgents and militias sought to gain and sustain control of civilians through propaganda, intimidation, assassinations of government officials and brutal killings of suspected informers. They also generated revenue through protection rackets linked to criminal groups and corrupt officials – as seen in the Taliban's taxes on narcotics producers and traders.

Understanding

It took years for the US and its allies to sufficiently understand both conflicts. This not only reduced their effectiveness but also increased resentment among the Iraqi and Afghan people, with negative implications from the strategic to the tactical level. Failure to properly handle detainees was the worst example of this; it not only squandered valuable intelligence opportunities but also greatly damaged the legitimacy of the Coalition.

The Coalition made significant efforts to improve its intelligence and surveillance capabilities. In the later parts of both wars, these improvements had a considerable effect. Just as important were attempts to improve understanding of culture and local politics, reflecting the profoundly human nature of the wars.

Understanding for regime change

Before 2001, the US and many of its allies believed that fully exploiting new technology required integrating the previously separate capabilities of intelligence, surveillance, target acquisition and reconnaissance to reduce the time between detecting targets and engaging them with precision weapons. This belief was at the core of the arguments put forward by advocates of the Revolution in Military Affairs.

In September 2001, the US and its allies had little actionable intelligence on Afghanistan, the Taliban or al-Qaeda. This shortfall stemmed from reductions in national strategic intelligence capability in the decade following the end of the Cold War. For example, between 1990 and 2001, both the CIA and the United Kingdom's Secret Intelligence Service reduced their personnel numbers by 25%.[3] This gap was bridged with help from Russia and a near-total concentration of US civilian- and military-intelligence assets on Afghanistan. But it was only after CIA and special-operations forces (SOF) teams linked up with warlords and militia commanders on the ground that the US gained the understanding to synchronise airstrikes with operations by Northern Alliance ground troops.

The limitations of ISTAR from the air were demonstrated in March 2002 during *Operation Anaconda*, which sought to encircle and destroy a major concentration of al-Qaeda forces near Afghanistan's border with Pakistan. US troops ran into unexpectedly heavy opposition from al-Qaeda fighters in previously undetected, well-prepared defensive positions. The operation also suffered from inadequate intelligence and air–land integration, insufficient organic fire support and over-reliance on warlord militias.[4]

In early 2002, most US intelligence capabilities were moved from Afghanistan to Iraq. Planners were also able to take advantage of 12 years of previous US and UK air operations in northern and southern Iraq, allowing them to assemble an adequate high-level intelligence picture of Iraqi conventional forces. Human Intelligence (HUMINT) was much less well developed.

Unsurprisingly, the air campaign generally had access to sufficient intelligence, which helped to keep civilian casualties and collateral damage to a minimum. But US ground troops advancing towards Baghdad were surprised by previously undetected Iraqi conventional ground troops.[5] Unexpectedly heavy Iraqi air defences contributed to the failure of a deep-strike attack by a US Army aviation brigade. Assaults by irregular forces in civilian vehicles and clothing came as a complete surprise.

Understanding for stabilisation

Initially, Coalition forces conducting stabilisation operations struggled to acquire intelligence. The advanced surveillance systems that had worked so well against Iraqi conventional forces were of little use against irregulars who blended into the civilian population.

International forces initially lacked sufficient linguists and translators. Local Afghans or Iraqis could be hired, but could not be security vetted and were vulnerable to intimidation. It took several years to vet and recruit enough military and contract interpreters.

Coalition forces initially had inadequate levels of cultural awareness, as could be seen in the use of sniffer dogs to search

Iraqi homes. This tactic had worked in Bosnia and Kosovo, but Iraqi Muslims felt that introducing 'unclean' beasts into their homes was deeply humiliating. The US and its allies gradually incorporated such cultural factors into their pre-tour preparation and training. Specialist cultural advisers were deployed, in some cases down to battalion level, and the UK formed a specialist unit of such experts.[6] The US Army identified a need to achieve a more granular understanding of the Iraqi people and their power structures, key relationships, customs and attitudes. To achieve this, it recruited specialist human-terrain teams, which included anthropologists and social scientists. Such experts were also recruited in Afghanistan.

Previous counter-insurgency (COIN) campaigns had shown that the local population was a principal source of intelligence, provided that security forces gained their trust and confidence. This required an expansion and decentralisation of intelligence organisations. As this lesson was rediscovered and applied, intelligence staffs greatly increased at all levels. HUMINT has been a decisive factor in all successful counter-insurgency campaigns, but has always taken years to develop. By 2007 in Iraq and 2010 in Afghanistan, it was starting to produce significant operational results.

The two wars coincided with the global expansion of the internet and social media. Monitoring information and opinions online provided insight into the thinking of the civilian population, and platforms such as Twitter could provide near-real-time information about security incidents. By mid-2013, the International Security Assistance Force (ISAF) Joint Command HQ in Kabul was using this resource.[7]

There were remarkable improvements in the technical means of intelligence collection and analysis. For instance, there was a massive expansion in intelligence gathering from airborne systems. Both manned and unmanned aircraft played a role in this. Surveillance systems fitted to masts and balloons above bases complemented these capabilities. Commanders and their intelligence staffs became increasingly connected to secure networks, requiring increasing bandwidth. Growing computer processing power enabled new techniques for fusing and analysing intelligence and surveillance data, as seen in the use of civilian law-enforcement analytical software to map insurgent networks.[8]

As the intelligence architecture in both theatres developed and matured, the ability to understand insurgent networks and generate intelligence that enabled attacks on key individuals greatly improved.[9] Material seized from insurgents included mobile phones, video recordings, computers and hard drives, as well as paper documents. Thus, forensic-investigation skills became essential to military intelligence. The US also deployed biometric systems in the field so that patrols, checkpoints and forces conducting arrest operations could rapidly identify civilians.

International forces progressively integrated tactical intelligence with national strategic intelligence capabilities. For example, by 2008, US divisions in Iraq had established intelligence-fusion centres at which the tactical intelligence they had developed was combined with US national signals intelligence. In Basra and Helmand, the British employed Operational Intelligence Support Groups, which provided tactical headquarters with national strategic intelligence.

None of this adaptation was smooth or easy. US conventional forces had little background in counter-insurgency and even less in the necessary intelligence capabilities. While the British had relevant experience from colonial campaigns and Northern Ireland, many necessary skills had atrophied. British forces were slower to adapt than their US counterparts in a number of important areas, such as fielding unmanned aerial vehicles (UAVs), and they failed to develop an adequate tactical-intelligence database in Iraq.

The British found that establishing an adequate ISTAR capability for their forces in Afghanistan required not only more collection systems, analysts and bandwidth, but also a change of approach. Previously, British ISTAR capability tended to be acquired and directed from the top down. To maximise ISTAR support for COIN operations, the UK began 'inverting the pyramid', or prioritising tactical support for tactical forces.[10]

The successful fusion of intelligence could allow for a high tempo of strike operations against insurgent commanders or logistics capabilities. If these efforts yielded further intelligence, they could spur subsequent strike operations. This became known as 'find, fix, finish, exploit, analyse and disseminate' (F3EAD). SOF effectively applied F3EAD in attacks on insurgent networks and, as the wars progressed, conventional forces increasingly adopted the approach.

Detainees and interrogation

In previous COIN operations, detainees had been important sources of intelligence. Detaining suspected militants reduced the insurgent threat without killing anyone. But captured personnel had to be properly handled; this included observing the Geneva Conventions, domestic law and any relevant emergency powers. In Iraq and Afghanistan, US and UK forces were slow to relearn the principles of prisoner and detainee handling. Early failures to apply this principle inflicted significant strategic damage on the legitimacy of the US and international forces in both wars.

Iraqi prisoners taken in *Operation Desert Storm* had been released quickly. During UN and NATO operations in Bosnia and Kosovo, international forces were not at war with local forces, so they detained few people – and quickly released those who were detained. Indicted war criminals captured by NATO SOF were passed to the international detention facility at the Hague War Crimes Tribunal. Therefore, there had been a minimal requirement to hold prisoners.

Contrary to popular film and television portrayals, extracting information from detainees requires properly trained and qualified interrogators, competent guard forces and expert linguists. Before a sufficient number of these personnel could be amassed, which took some time, detainees in US and British custody were abused by inadequately trained and supervised guards. In early 2004, the international media spread images of US abuses at Abu Ghraib prison, causing immense damage to the legitimacy of the country – not only in Iraq and the wider Muslim world, but globally.

American and British forces appeared to have collectively forgotten the potential intelligence value of properly and humanely handling prisoners. Along with a lack of command attention, this may explain why both US and UK forces made insufficient arrangements for the detention and interrogation of detainees in Iraq. The abuses committed by US troops at Abu Ghraib and by British troops on at least two occasions in southern Iraq primarily resulted from inadequate resources, training and planning, as well as poor leadership and the neglect of basic principles. In the British case, it appears that planning for prisoner handling began too late. A 2013 independent inquiry into UK troops' mistreatment of detainees in Iraq concluded that 'failures to maintain adequate prisoner of war handling and interrogation doctrine led directly to inadequate prisoner of war handling guidance being issued in the lead up to the warfighting phase'.[11] The abuses acted as a recruitment tool for militias and insurgents.

Once these incidents came to light, both countries initiated remedial action. For example, in Iraq and Afghanistan, the US found it necessary to greatly increase the resources allocated to detention facilities. Just as important were the appointment of a senior officer to command detainee operations and measures taken to increase the number of properly trained interrogators. This was a slow process, but as the quantity and quality of interrogators increased in both countries, so did the flow of actionable intelligence.

The Joint Special Operations Command (JSOC) ran its own detention facilities for personnel captured during its raids. General Stanley McChrystal, its commander, wrote:

> Detainees can explain the meaning of what we see from other intelligence sources and can let us step into the mechanics, mindset and weaknesses of the enemy organization. Detainees, whether they talk out of fear, because they think its pointless not to, or because their egos can be manipulated and played, can reveal not just what the enemy thinks, but *how* he thinks and *why* he fights.
>
> Detainee operations were as difficult and sensitive as they were vital. The resources required and the complexities associated with them caused most organizations to avoid such duty … I was one of the leaders who lacked experience in detainee custody and exploitation. I had studied history and understood the theory but had never done anything remotely like running a prison. My peers and subordinates were similarly positioned.[12]

Leaders needed to make greater effort to ensure that the detention regime and facilities met the high standards of understandably nervous governments. For instance, McChrystal improved the detention facility, its leadership and the mindset of his force, particularly by using 'mature seasoned leaders' rather than individual reinforcements from outside JSOC to run the detention operation. And, after initially supporting 'enhanced interrogation techniques including sleep management', he came to view these practices as wrong.

The vast majority of people detained by US forces in Iraq and Afghanistan were held in US detention facilities in the respective country. In mid-2007, US detention facilities held more than 27,000 people in Iraq alone. Detainees were regularly released, but largely on a 'first in, first out' basis. Some insurgents were arrested and set free on multiple occasions, a practice US troops referred to as 'catch and release' – a sport-fishing phrase.

Although the US troops conducting the arrests met the minimum legal requirements, the detention facilities were becoming recruiting grounds for insurgents. There was no segregation of hard-core activists and other detainees, which allowed the insurgents to impose their will on other prisoners through murder and other violence, and to actively recruit and train detainees. The number of al-Qaeda operatives in detention facilities grew quickly due to the 2007 US surge and SOF operations.

An active al-Qaeda insurgency in Camp Bucca, the main US detention facility, led to increasing violence, including attacks on US guards. After a riot involving 10,000 detainees nearly became a mass breakout, the US decided to conduct 'counter-insurgency operations inside the wire'. This required not only an improved guard force, but also the separation of the hard-core insurgents from the rest of the prison population. Complementary efforts were made to develop a robust and transparent process that allowed for the release of detainees who were assessed to no longer pose a threat. American forces introduced a rehabilitation and reintegration scheme, which included literacy programmes and paid work for 'reconcilable

Pointers to future conflict: understanding

- COIN campaigns require armed forces to expand and decentralise intelligence capabilities.
- Technological advances are no substitute for the human component of understanding, including linguistic skills, cultural empathy and the unique role of human intelligence. Because war is essentially a human activity, these capabilities are likely to remain as important as technical ISTAR capacity.
- Specific ISTAR adaptations – including the many applications of UAVs, the use of sophisticated intelligence-fusion techniques and building human-intelligence networks – are likely to have wider relevance in future conflicts.
- Detainees and prisoners will continue to be totemic issues for all parties to armed conflict, and will probably play a major role in the contest for narrative and legitimacy. All military personnel must have a thorough understanding of the Geneva Conventions and other relevant legislation, as well as the values that underpin them.
- In future conflicts, it will be essential to deploy capable prisoner- and detainee-handling organisations, as well as the qualified and trained interrogators necessary to generate intelligence, from the outset.
- It will also be necessary to use incentives to prevent insurgencies developing within detention facilities, and to be able to release reformed detainees back into society. Prisoners and detainees must be treated not as liabilities but as potential assets that provide opportunities.

detainees'. The initiative was largely successful: graduates of the rehabilitation programme at Camp Bucca had a recidivism rate of less than 1%.[13]

By 2009, Washington and NATO were seeking to transfer the vast majority of detainees to Iraq's and Afghanistan's authorities. Both countries' judicial apparatus and correctional facilities had fallen below modern international standards even before 9/11, and the turmoil immediately after regime change had further degraded them. As a consequence, the transfer required considerable multi-agency activity in rebuilding and modernising these systems.

The US transferred its remaining detainees to the Iraqi authorities before its 2011 withdrawal. In Afghanistan, many troop-contributing countries faced the problem that a significant number of Afghan prisons failed to meet the minimum requirements in their domestic law. For example, UK human-rights legislation laid out standards of treatment for detainees, including the right not to be tortured. This meant that there were times when UK detainees could not be transferred to some Afghan prisons.

International military capability
Stabilisation: operations and tactics
The conflicts in Afghanistan and Iraq ranged from low-level firefights, ambushes and roadside bomb attacks to corps operations involving several divisions. In both countries, US and allied forces combined infantry, armour and engineers to attack insurgent strongholds. They employed combined-arms tactics honed in twentieth-century wars, complemented by new capabilities such as precision attack using artillery, missiles, helicopters, fighters and UAVs, as well as reconstruction, development and information operations.

Whenever they concentrated sufficient troops in an area of Afghanistan or Iraq for long enough, international and indigenous forces successfully applied the COIN approach described in the 2006 US Army manual FM 3–24. The density of forces on the ground was a key factor. Initially, the Coalition only achieved adequate density on occasion, such as in the assault on Falluja and the COIN operations in Al-Qaim, Tal Afar and Ramadi. The 2007 surge was able to concentrate sufficient forces in key areas in and around Baghdad. Even so, the operation had to be sequenced.

In Afghanistan, ISAF was able to employ similar approaches. Provided that there were sufficient international or Afghan forces to hold areas that had been cleared, similar results were achieved. The same applied in Kabul, where by 2013 the Afghan police had taken charge of security and several outer rings of layered defences.[14]

In both wars, common factors in successful US and NATO clearance operations included the concentration of sufficient airborne-surveillance and -strike capability, as well as adequate ground forces to manoeuvre, clear and then hold captured terrain. Where the terrain permitted, these forces would include tanks and armoured or protected infantry. Integration with influence operations and tactical reconstruction were essential to these efforts.[15]

It was also important for such operations to involve indigenous forces – providing a 'local face' for building empathy with the civil population – as well as physical barriers and permanent checkpoints that could restrict insurgent movements and protect cleared areas.

Firepower and manoeuvre

Stabilisation operations required interaction with the local population. Due to the need to operate in the heavily populated areas of Iraq and Afghanistan, and the mountainous terrain of eastern Afghanistan, infantry became the key ground-combat capability.

As there was much more dismounted close combat than anticipated, international forces made an effort to upgrade infantry effectiveness. This involved a revival of sniper tactics, aided by new rifles, night sights and handheld laser range finders. But such enhancements did not produce a decisive increase in effectiveness, as the weight of body armour and other equipment greatly slowed troops.

Although many Taliban and Iraqi armoured vehicles were destroyed by missiles and bombs from fixed-wing aircraft and helicopters, US and UK tanks and armoured vehicles played a decisive role in the removal of Iraqi President Saddam Hussein. With their unique combination of firepower, mobility and protection, tanks and armoured infantry fighting vehicles had great utility. Their advanced armour conferred a high degree of immunity to rocket-propelled grenades. US and UK armoured columns were able to outmanoeuvre Iraqi defenders, even in urban areas.

In stabilisation operations, tanks and other armoured vehicles supported infantry and fought insurgents, rather than fighting other tanks. Firepower from armoured vehicles was invaluable, as was intimate tactical cooperation between armoured vehicles and dismounted infantry. The tank's heavy gun provided a unique capability for attacking bunkers and buildings.

Second only to protecting themselves, armies sought to protect the population around them by minimising collateral damage and civilian casualties. This required restrictive rules of engagement, complemented by precision weapons such as guided artillery shells and rockets, including the US Guided Multiple Launch Rocket System. The British rushed the Israeli *Spike* non-line-of-sight missile into service. Named *Exactor*, this system had the advantage of putting a soldier in the loop throughout its flight, which made it particularly useful for attacking fleeing targets in populated areas. The employment of munitions with small warheads such the *Hellfire* missile – which became the weapon of choice for US UAVs – supplemented these developments. The combination of greatly improved intelligence capabilities and precision weapons was decisive in its own right, whether a strike was delivered by a bomb, a missile or an SOF raid.

Protection

Tactical ground combat was often as intense as it was in the Second World War, the Korean War or the Vietnam War. As the popularity of the conflicts in Afghanistan and Iraq declined in troop-contributing nations, protection and protective equipment became a much higher priority than had been envisaged beforehand.

International forces increasingly sought protection for ground vehicles. Armoured vehicles were fitted with additional armour, remotely operated weapons and electronic countermeasures that could jam radio-command links to roadside bombs. This increased the size and weight of vehicles such as the UK's *Warrior*, which grew from 27 tonnes to 40tn. As part of the initiative, US and allied forces rapidly procured around 28,000 wheeled, protected patrol vehicles optimised to protect their passengers from roadside bombs, such as the US mine-resistant ambush-protected (MRAP) vehicle.

In both wars, IEDs were responsible for the majority of US and allied casualties. An arms race developed between the increasingly advanced efforts of insurgent and militia IED experts and allied counter-IED capability. International forces spent billions of dollars on improving capabilities for detecting and neutralising IEDs, which became a core activity for all deployed troops. This ranged from equipping all infantry with handheld detectors to deploying sophisticated battalion-sized counter-IED task forces that used advanced equipment. There was increasing convergence between general combat-engineering capabilities and specialist explosive-ordnance disposal (EOD) skills. This could be seen in southern Afghanistan in 2010, as the US Marine Corps (USMC) and the British Army made extensive use of engineer tanks to breach high-density IED belts.

Most of the armies that deployed to Iraq and Afghanistan also increasingly used unmanned ground vehicles (UGVs). Initially, most of these were remotely operated EOD systems. The number of US UGVs rose from 162 in 2004 to around 12,000 in 2012, while the US and the UK also developed the ability to remotely operate previously manned vehicles. These included excavators and a lightly armoured 4×4 vehicle to mount ground-penetrating radar that could detect buried IEDs.

Some insurgent technological innovations could be countered by technology such as detectors, jammers and improved armour. But technical responses took time to work out. In the meantime, commanders could only adjust their tactics, techniques and procedures. In reaction to the fielding in 2005 of EFP roadside bombs, which overmatched the protection of all armoured vehicles operated by the Coalition, US and UK troops adjusted their tactics to reduce vulnerability as they developed additional armour and new countermeasures. But some insurgent innovations had no technological counter.

The IED threat could be largely circumvented by moving troops using aircraft. Many countries bought more helicopters, and there was a revival in the supply of isolated units by parachute drops. However, not even the US had enough helicopters to move all its troops and supplies by air, so protective armour and jammers were also added to logistic vehicles.

Dealing with insurgent attacks on Coalition airfields and bases, which involved indirect fire from rockets and mortars, required a similar mixture of technology and tactics. American and British forces used radars to provide warnings of such attacks and, in Iraq, adapted *Phalanx* naval guns to intercept incoming munitions. They also employed counter-battery fire but, as the enemy could neutralise this using timers, the effort was probably counterproductive. In 2008 the US used UAVs, attack helicopters and fixed-wing aircraft to combat rocket attacks on the Green Zone from Sadr City.

These initiatives to counter IEDs and indirect fire were essentially defensive. It was important to complement such defensive measures with intelligence-led strike operations to disrupt the networks that directed, supplied and supported insurgent activities. But, unless there were sufficient troops and aircraft to dominate the ground and deter rocket and mortar teams, as well as the placement of IEDs, the insurgents had the initiative.

Airpower

Air superiority provided international forces with a major asymmetric advantage, as they had the ability to attack enemies anywhere in Afghanistan or Iraq with bombs, missiles or helicopter-borne ground troops and SOF. Regime change in Afghanistan depended on the deployment of CIA personnel and SOF by helicopters flying at long range in mountainous terrain. Some SOF and supplies were delivered by parachute. ISAF was deployed to Kabul by air transport, and it was sustained by air until logistics lines of communication from Pakistan and Central Asia were opened.

Fighter support for troops in Afghanistan came from air bases in Central Asia, as well as Bagram and Kandahar airfields. US-led forces in Iraq relied on fighters based throughout the Gulf and at Balad, a US base north of Baghdad. Aircraft were also surged from US carriers. International forces based attack and transport helicopters throughout both countries, with the former increasingly employed to escort the latter. Manned and unmanned aircraft became ever more important to ISTAR operations. Large long-endurance aircraft such as the US Navy's P-3 *Orion* and the Royal Air Force's *Nimrod* proved to be especially useful as ISTAR platforms.

In both countries, it was necessary to employ airpower at a low tactical level. For example, the intense fighting in southern and eastern Afghanistan required aerial firepower to break up Taliban assaults. This close air support was routinely delivered by attack helicopters, fighter-bombers and strategic bombers. Without satellite communications, helicopter resupply and direct support from attack helicopters and precision bombing, the isolated British bases in Helmand Province would have probably fallen to attacks by hundreds of determined Taliban fighters in 2006.

Both wars required ever-closer tactical air–land integration, and wider efforts to field the specialist parties and communications necessary to achieve this. By 2006, the US and NATO routinely deployed tactical air-control parties at company level and often below, while integrating armed UAVs into the ground tactical battle. This was a higher degree of air–land integration than had ever been achieved by land forces.

Insurgent groups were occasionally able to down low-flying transport aircraft and helicopters. Coalition and ISAF forces fitted manned aircraft with defensive-aid suites designed to jam or decoy missile-guidance systems. This meant that few manned aircraft (of any type) were lost – far fewer than in the Vietnam War, for instance.

Contractor support

To reduce the number of troops deployed in stabilisation operations, international forces made extensive use of contractors to deliver supplies to military bases. Local 'jingly' trucks operated by civilian hauliers carried all the equipment and supplies that travelled from the Pakistani port of Karachi to major US and NATO bases in Afghanistan. There was also wide use of contract civilian air freighters and, to a lesser extent, contract helicopters that could supply isolated bases.

As the wars progressed, civilian contractors took on other logistic roles. At the British base at Camp Bastion, in Iraq, contractors provided catering, repair and support equipment, and maintained UAVs. Krauss-Maffei Wegmann deployed technicians to maintain German armoured vehicles in the Afghan city of Mazar-i-Sharif.

The US used contractors to provide security for civilian officials. Although this reduced the number of troops required, the aggressive behaviour and apparently minimal rules of engagement displayed by contract personnel led to Iraqi and Afghan civilian casualties. Other nations were reluctant to use private security companies to assist with armed guarding.

Medical support

The two wars saw considerable advances in battlefield medicine, including the fielding of anticoagulant bandages and the deployment of military paramedics at the platoon and squad levels. Due to increasing numbers of dedicated casualty-evacuation helicopters carrying military paramedics, more casualties were able to reach surgery within an hour of being wounded.

Pointers to future conflict: combat capabilities

- Airpower provided a decisive asymmetric advantage to US and international forces. Air forces and armies work best in a land campaign when their actions are fully synchronised.
- In 'operations among the people' involving counter-insurgency or other forms of conflict, success can depend on the concentration of air and land forces (including tanks, armoured or protected infantry, and armoured engineers) and the integration of tactical action with information operations and tactical reconstruction.
- Infantry are likely to continue to be a key combat capability, especially in urban areas, close country and mountainous terrain, but improvements to infantry protection greatly restrict mobility.
- Many armoured vehicles and their modifications are likely to be valuable in future conflicts.
- Artillery will likely remain useful, with unguided artillery increasingly complemented by guided shells and

rockets, as well as emerging 'man in the loop' indirect-fire precision-attack capabilities.
- Direct-fire, indirect-fire and air-delivered precision weapons are likely to be increasingly valuable. They will be dependent on precision ISTAR, but will offer opportunities to reduce civilian casualties and collateral damage.
- Although the use of contractors in stabilisation operations is likely to continue, it will require a proper framework of command, rules of engagement and legal accountability. This should ensure that contractors' conduct meets the same standards of force protection and behaviour as the troops of the country that employs them.
- In peacetime, military medical and welfare organisations must be designed to expand to accommodate potential future casualty rates, and to be capable of adapting to new and unforeseen challenges.

Field hospitals became more advanced than those in previous wars, forward deploying technology such as CAT scanners. Improved electronic links, including video conferencing, improved integration with hospitals in troop-contributing countries. And medical-evacuation aircraft carried advanced life-support equipment and experts to operate it.[16]

Therefore, a greater proportion of troops survived wounds that would have been fatal in previous campaigns. This created unexpected challenges in the rehabilitation and recovery of casualties, as well as their long-term support. The military authorities had not anticipated that they would have to deal with so many badly wounded personnel and their families. The development stretched military arrangements in the UK and the US Department of Veterans Affairs almost to breaking point. In the UK, this damaged the credibility of the armed forces and the Ministry of Defence.[17]

Special-operations forces

Elite forces trained for especially difficult missions are as old as armies themselves. In the twentieth century, SOF had a multitude of roles, but their core tasks were usually operations in enemy territory, supporting indigenous forces, hostage rescue and counter-terrorism. They were widely employed in these roles in Afghanistan and Iraq, adapting their capabilities and operational approaches.

Much media reporting and analysis of SOF mixes snippets of fact with vast quantities of speculation. Indeed, the media has paid disproportionate attention to accounts by those few former personnel who have publicised their stories – sometimes for money, sometimes to settle old scores.[18] However, there is enough publicly available authoritative material to identify and analyse the key roles of SOF in both wars.

In 2001 SOF decisively energised the militias of the Northern Alliance and coordinated their attacks with US airpower. They were greatly aided by the CIA, demonstrating the value of close cooperation between SOF and intelligence agencies across the spectrum of conflict. In 2003 US, UK and Australian SOF swept across western Iraq from Jordan to distract and deceive Iraqi forces, while denying Iraq the opportunity to fire *Scud* missiles at Israel, as it had in 1991. These operations saw SOF adopt one of their classic roles: operating in small parties at long range in difficult terrain and independently of conventional ground forces, but closely integrated with airpower.

Subsequent operations against insurgent networks in Iraq and Afghanistan were conducted from fixed bases, with unconstrained access to secure bandwidth. The most difficult missions involved entering territory controlled by the enemy, such as the numerous UK SOF raids into areas of Afghanistan controlled by the Taliban. The most secretive and elite US SOF units were grouped together in JSOC, commanded by McChrystal between October 2003 and June 2008. Most of JSOC's efforts involved raids against al-Qaeda insurgent networks, especially commanders and bomb-makers.

Initially, inadequate integration of JSOC's various components limited its effectiveness. The organisation was also constrained by command-and-control arrangements: while Central Command (CENTCOM) was responsible for conventional military operations in Afghanistan and Iraq, Special Operations Command (SOCOM) – of which JSOC is a part – led the fight against al-Qaeda on the military side. Both commands answer directly to the US secretary of defence. Independently, the CIA also used its intelligence-gathering and direct-action assets, including armed UAVs and paramilitaries, to counter al-Qaeda.

McChrystal spent much time working to overcome these sub-optimal strategic command-and-control arrangements, personally coordinating JSOC's activities with CENTCOM's conventional forces and seeking to better integrate the two. He reached out to US intelligence agencies, particularly the CIA, to increase JSOC's ability to develop targeting intelligence. At the same time, he made greater use of airborne surveillance from both UAVs and manned aircraft, as well as US 'special reconnaissance' troops conducting plain-clothes surveillance.

JSOC combined intelligence from interrogations with information drawn from the full range of its intelligence and surveillance capabilities, such as those for rapidly analysing captured documents, computers and telephones.[19] This allowed the organisation to improve its decision-making and tempo to better attack al-Qaeda's networks. JSOC preferred to capture insurgents and seize their paraphernalia for intelligence exploitation, which identified further targets and in turn maintained pressure on insurgent networks. As the balance shifted in favour of the US and Iraqi forces, JSOC devoted an increasing proportion of its efforts to countering the threat from armed Shia extremists, many of whom were supported by Iran. As part of this, the organisation increasingly worked with Iraqi SOF.

The number of NATO SOF in Afghanistan increased with ISAF's expansion in 2006, and again from 2009 onwards as the US transferred SOF from Iraq. Their principal role was attacking Taliban and al-Qaeda commanders, as well as key figures such as bomb-makers. In doing so, they applied the same approaches as in Iraq, particularly in the development of actionable intelligence. By 2010, there were a considerable number of raids every night. As in Iraq, they increasingly operated alongside host-nation SOF. But the night raids were unpopular with the Afghan people – who felt humiliated by this intrusion into their homes – and drew repeated public criticism from the Afghan president. Lacking an easy solution to this problem, NATO SOF increasingly transferred responsibility for the raids to their Afghan counterparts from 2011 onwards (Afghan-led raids provoked far less criticism).

There was a lack of SOF to fulfil the requirements of US commanders in Iraq and Afghanistan. US SOF relinquished much of their traditional foreign internal-defence role to conventional forces. The USMC was persuaded to create a new SOF, and US SOF acquired additional UAVs and manned surveillance aircraft. By 2008, SOCOM had a strength of 55,000 troops, a 30% increase since 2001.[20] The UK also expanded its SOF, fielding a dedicated Special Forces Support Group based on a parachute battalion – which fulfilled a similar function to the US Army Rangers – while increasing the number of its dedicated helicopters and intelligence personnel.

The SOF of many other US allies faced similar pressures from 9/11 onwards. But SOF commanders were anxious to maintain the demanding selection and training processes that prepared their personnel for the most dangerous missions. They worried that increasing numbers at the expense of quality would lower overall effectiveness. Indeed, in some forces, this turned out to be the case.

Integration of SOF and conventional forces

For the first part of both wars, there was little or no coordination between conventional ground forces and SOF. Units often received little or no warning of SOF raids in their areas of responsibility and were usually left to manage the consequences – not least collateral damage, civilian casualties and antagonised local populations. For example, the Taliban exploited an unsuccessful US–Afghan SOF raid in Garmser in January 2010 by claiming that a Koran had been deliberately desecrated in the operation. Skilful Taliban agitation triggered riots against US and Afghan forces, resulting in the deaths of six Afghan civilians. The situation was only resolved after extensive negotiations, by which time the district governor's political position had been severely damaged.[21]

Conventional-force commanders often complained about the apparently generous allocation of scarce ISTAR resources to SOF. Coordination between SOF and conventional forces improved over time – not least due to the efforts of SOF commanders to reach out to their counterparts in conventional forces – as they increasingly reinforced the success of each other's operations. As US and Iraqi conventional ground forces cleared key terrain in and around Baghdad during the surge, surviving insurgents were forced to withdraw to unfamiliar areas and to adjust what was left of their networks. This increased their visibility to US surveillance, providing additional intelligence for SOF attacks, which in turn aided subsequent clearance operations by conventional forces, creating a positive feedback loop. In southern Afghanistan in 2009–10, SOF attacks on insurgent leaders preceded deliberate clearance operations by UK, US and Afghan conventional forces.[22]

A major problem in Afghanistan was that, during most of the conflict there, the senior US commander did not control all American SOF. However, the eventual creation of a single Combined Forces Special Operations Component Command rationalised the US chain of command.

Iran's Quds Force: an alternative approach to SOF

Iran made extensive use of the Quds Force to raise the cost of the Iraq War for the US, and to increase its influence with Iraqi Shi'ites. This elite force not only fulfilled many of the same roles as Western SOF, but also had the Iranian government's policy

Pointers to future conflict: special-operations forces

- SOF continued to have very high utility, both operating in small parties at long range and integrated with conventional forces conducting COIN.
- SOF will need to retain the ability to integrate ISTAR and intelligence analysis in developing targets, as well as in working with integral special-reconnaissance and supporting infantry.
- SOF will remain valuable in supporting and influencing indigenous forces in territory that conventional forces cannot or should not reach.
- Inter-agency cooperation is as important to SOF operations as it is to conventional operations.

lead for Iraq, Syria and Lebanon. For instance, it was revealed in 2008 that the Iranian ambassador to Iraq was a Quds Force officer. The organisation acted as a conduit for funding, training and advice to special groups of Shia militias, improving their capability to attack Coalition forces. It also appears to have helped plan a January 2007 operation in which militants successfully impersonated US officers to kidnap American personnel from a US–Iraqi joint security station at Karbala.

There was considerable evidence that Quds Force operatives were active in Iraq, particularly in documents seized in SOF raids. These raids helped counter the Quds Force's influence by detaining some of its personnel and producing hard evidence of its activities, which the US used to persuade Iraqi Prime Minister Nuri al-Maliki to tackle Iran. Nonetheless, the US had limited options in this situation, as it was in no position to attack Iran directly without greatly increasing the strategic risk to its forces in Iraq, the Gulf and Afghanistan.

By supporting Shia extremist groups, Iran waged a proxy war against the US and the UK in Iraq. Aside from increasing the cost of the war and Tehran's influence in Iraq, this served as a form of indirect deterrence against a US-led regime-change attack on Iran. The Iranian leadership probably regards the investment in the Quds Force and its operations to support and influence Shia militants as successful.

Building local military capability

To pass security leadership to the Afghan and Iraqi authorities, international forces needed to build up their indigenous security forces. Before 9/11, the US experience of 'foreign internal defence' largely resided in SOF. Many Coalition and NATO nations had considerable experience of security-sector reform in the Balkans, Africa, Latin America and Asia. This experience had shown the task to be an inherently multi-agency activity that required initiatives not only to train and equip armies, police forces and intelligence services, but also to rebuild and reform judicial systems and security ministries, as well as establish top-level mechanisms for managing security, such as national-security councils.

Thus, the US and many of its allies knew what they needed to do in Iraq and Afghanistan, but it proved much more difficult than anticipated. Initial efforts to create new forces for both countries were given insufficient resources and inadequate leadership. In both countries, air-force capacity-building started too late. In 2014 the collapse of Iraqi forces facing an attack by the Islamic State, also known as ISIS or ISIL, showed how corruption and politicisation eroded effectiveness.

In Afghanistan and Iraq, initial capacity-building efforts concentrated on volume at the expense of quality, to operationalise indigenous forces as quickly as possible. Capacity-building in relevant ministries (defence for the armed forces, interior for the police) and necessary logistics and training infrastructure began later.

This sequencing was understandable, but the risks it involved were exposed during Iraqi Army operations after the 2007 surge – in which weaknesses in high-level Iraqi command, control and logistics constrained increasingly capable and confident Iraqi combat forces. This suggests that full-spectrum security-sector reform requires such capacities to be generated in parallel with combat capability rather than as an after-thought.

In Afghanistan, as the size and capability of indigenous forces increased, the creation of infrastructure and institutions became more important. Even as the Afghan surge ended and the number of ISAF mentors with front-line forces declined, the US and NATO retained mentors and advisers in the Afghan ministries of defence and interior.

Capacity-building in Iraq

The transition strategy in Iraq depended on building the country's security capability. Initial efforts to raise local security forces were tested in the 2004 Shia uprisings and the operations to stabilise Falluja, exposing considerable limitations and weaknesses resulting from a shortage of time, resources and command priorities.

Iraq's army and police SOF, supported by US SOF mentors and ISTAR, became increasingly capable as the war continued, but US SOF had no spare capacity to assist with building Iraqi conventional forces. Initial US efforts to provide military trainers were not given priority, and were further inhibited by a lack of US Army experience of capacity-building. With the 2004 formation of Multi-National Security Transition Command–Iraq, command focus and resources improved. The enterprise was conducted on a huge scale: it involved the creation of recruit-training organisations; schools for all branches of the Iraqi armed forces; basic and advanced officer schools; a staff college; and a massive US-led equipment programme. All this required coordination and synchronisation to ensure that new units and formations were based on properly trained personnel with the right equipment.

The US embedded Military Transition Teams (MiTTs) in all Iraqi units and formations. These small teams of US military personnel living, working and fighting with indigenous security forces' units and headquarters were tasked with improving Iraqi capability as operations took place. They provided not only mentoring, advice and liaison with Coalition units, but also Coalition capabilities, including airpower, fire support, medical evacuation and logistics. This helped the Iraqis climb the necessarily steep learning curve in improving their operational effectiveness under fire, to make them capable of conducting independent operations. The teams also provided the Coalition with accurate information on the Iraqi forces' operations and capabilities.

The UK chose not to adopt this approach, partly as it felt it had insufficient resources to supply the same level of force protection. As the threat in southern Iraq increased, the resources devoted to force protection reduced the effort to assist Iraqi forces in the area. This meant that the UK approach to developing the Iraqi forces (form, train and equip) was less effective than the US approach (form, train, equip, mentor, partner and recognise that 'your fight is our fight').

The weaknesses of the British approach were exposed in the early stages of *Operation Charge of the Knights*, in which un-mentored Iraqi troops performed poorly. The British had failed to establish as strong an empathetic relationship with the Iraqis as had the Americans, suggesting that it is more effective to build indigenous security capacity through active support than by passively promoting self-reliance.[23]

Capacity-building in Afghanistan
In early 2002, international forces reached a broad agreement on the need to rebuild the Afghan security forces. The difficulties of such an effort were even greater in Afghanistan than in Iraq, and were probably underestimated by the US and its allies. Afghanistan had little military capability other than the

Northern Alliance and warlords' militias, some of which were funded by the CIA. Additional handicaps included the relative lack of education and literacy in the general population.

Following successful practice in Iraq, the US and NATO deployed mentors to Afghan National Army formations and units. These Operational Mentor and Liaison Teams (OMLTs) played the same role as the MiTTs in Iraq.[24] But, until 2009, international efforts to develop the Afghan National Security Forces (ANSF) through mentoring, training and equipment programmes were insufficient to address the deteriorating security situation. In 2009, shortly after his appointment as ISAF commander, McChrystal emphasised building the capability of the ANSF, prompting the formation of the NATO Training Mission–Afghanistan and providing a significant boost to staff and resources.

McChrystal also applied the concept of 'embedded partnering'. This aimed to combine the two military forces into a single team, exploiting ISAF's combat power and technology and the ANSF's situational awareness. The concept applied at every echelon, from government ministries to patrols and checkpoints. For example, in 2010 an Afghan corps HQ took the lead in the third phase of *Operation Moshtarak*, and set-piece orders from Afghan rather than NATO commanders initiated the later phases of *Operation Hamkari*.

Militias
Fighting in the Tora Bora mountains and *Operation Anaconda*, in which militia members were often reluctant to risk their safety, revealed the limitations of US attempts to use local militias against the Taliban and al-Qaeda. Some warlords sought to remove personal opponents by manipulating the US, providing false intelligence that these opponents were Taliban or al-Qaeda remnants. This practice, along with predatory

behaviour by US-supported militias, contributed to growing support for the Taliban.

From 2002, the Afghan government, Japan and the US sought to reduce the number of informal militias. However, the nature of Afghan political and social structures meant that powerful figures would always be able to generate bands of loyal armed followers. Nonetheless, putting militias on the US or NATO payroll could enhance stability. This was a key factor in the US ability to manage, influence and control the Iraqi Sunni militias that changed sides to join the fight against al-Qaeda in 2006–07. The practice of co-opting militias also proved valuable in Afghanistan. For instance, in southern Helmand in 2009–12, it allowed district governors and some of their key allies to retain limited numbers of tribal bodyguards, thereby increasing their security, confidence and influence.[25] By paying the militias' wages, the US achieved a degree of influence and control over them, not least in limiting their growth and inhibiting their predatory behaviour. Over time, the US was also able to persuade many militia members to enlist in the Afghan police.

The Afghan Local Police programme saw detachments of US SOF embedded in locally raised self-defence forces. It sought to generate and sustain small self-defence forces in villages that opted to resist the Taliban in areas where there were few international or Afghan forces. It also exploited successful revolts against the Taliban by some villages, such as that in Gizab district, in Uruzgan Province. Described by US General David Petraeus as a 'community watch with AK47s', the programme was seen as a relatively cheap method of connecting the Afghan government to villages.

But, in both wars, co-opted militias also created risks, as they were prone to human-rights abuses and could slip back into predatory behaviour. Another weakness of such forces was their tendency to fall under the control of local warlords.

In Iraq, the US countered this by putting the Sons of Iraq on its payroll and gathering biometric data to discourage recidivism. Measures to avoid this in Afghanistan included gathering biometric data, as well as making the detachments answerable to a local, representative Shura and the district police chief.

Indigenous air forces: too little too late?

Before 2003, Iraq had a large air force, albeit one that had been greatly degraded by two wars. However, although Iraq had a relatively well-educated population to draw on for personnel with technical skills, it failed to sustain an indigenous air capability that could provide sufficient security. Fighting between Iraqi forces and ISIS in 2014 showed that, while the government had enough transport aircraft and helicopters to move troops around the country, its attack capability was limited to a few *Hind* helicopters and armed Cessna light attack aircraft. The delivery of Su-25 attack jets from Russia and Iran bridged this deficiency in the short term.

Developing an indigenous air force was an even greater challenge in Afghanistan than in Iraq, as the former country lacked the educated personnel with the English-language and technical skills needed to keep such a force flying. It appears that the decision to create an Afghan air force and to provide international support to build its capability was only taken in 2007. Afghanistan fielded a limited initial air-force capability in 2010, but this was vulnerable to corruption.

The US surge in Afghanistan sought to boost efforts to build an Afghan air force optimised for COIN. Although this would not be comparable to the considerable US and NATO air support available at the height of the war, it was intended to be sufficient for Kabul's long-term requirements, provided that COIN operations could make full use of the Afghan National

Army's other sources of fire support, especially mortars and artillery. Yet, as of late 2016, the Afghan Air Force had yet to achieve full capability, and was constrained by a shortage of educated and literate personnel.

Corruption and politicisation

Left unchecked, corruption can reduce the morale and cohesion of forces. It can degrade logistics, as war supplies are sold on the black market or money for fuel, food, water and other supplies is stolen.

After Coalition mentor teams observed corruption in Iraq, they brought it to the attention of the senior commander of the unit or formation. Although this sometimes addressed the problem, there was evidence that the more militarily effective an Iraqi unit, the more willing international mentors were to tolerate corruption within it. On a number of occasions, Iraqi units were withdrawn from operations for periods of retraining, providing an opportunity to dismiss corrupt and ineffective commanders.[26]

In Afghanistan, ISAF created Task Force–Shafafiyat to identify and reduce corruption, which in many cases had been exacerbated by contracts placed by the US and its allies. Adjustment of contracting processes helped address the issue, but much corruption in Kabul occurred at a high level, and it was often difficult to distinguish between corruption and political patronage.[27]

A related issue was the danger that indigenous forces could become excessively politicised. This was a major problem in Iraq from 2007 onwards, as Maliki exerted increasing control of Iraqi forces. Petraeus and other US leaders worried that this would allow him to use Iraqi forces to further a narrowly political and sectarian agenda rather than to meet the full security needs of Iraq. There were 'robust discussions' between

Pointers to future conflict: building indigenous forces

- Capacity-building is a core task for all militaries. It would be unwise to allow it to become the preserve of SOF.
- Embedding mentoring teams within indigenous forces is an effective way of providing active support, coordinating with international forces and building capability and confidence.
- Institutional reform of defence, security and interior ministries needs to be conducted in parallel with other efforts.
- It is essential to make co-opted militias accountable and deter recidivism or capture by local warlords.

- Efforts to build security capacity should not underestimate the importance of establishing air capability alongside army and police capability. Since this requires educated, literate and numerate personnel, it should be undertaken from the outset.
- Corruption in indigenous forces is best tackled through a comprehensive approach, including political, development and intelligence agencies. It is essential that international forces avoid actions that exacerbate corruption.

Petraeus, his successors and Maliki, but the US had only limited leverage, which decreased further after its 2011 withdrawal. Maliki assumed direct ministerial authority for the armed forces, police and intelligence agencies, leading to the replacement of tried and tested police and army commanders with less capable but politically loyal proxies. This greatly reduced the effectiveness and impartiality of the security forces, and appears to have been a significant factor in the collapse of Iraqi forces attacked by ISIS in 2014.

Conclusion

The clearance operations in Sadr City in 2008 and southern Afghanistan in 2009–11 are exemplars for future offensive operations among the people, including combat in urban areas, in COIN and other forms of conflict. They suggest that success in such efforts can stem from the concentration of sufficient air and land forces, including tanks, armoured or protected infantry and armoured engineers. The integration of tactical action with information operations and reconstruction is also essential.

Infantry are the most important combat capability in such operations, especially in urban areas and mountainous terrain. This is likely to continue to be the case, but the improvements to infantry protection made in the Afghan and Iraqi conflicts significantly restrict mobility. A wide range of armoured vehicles had a key role in both wars and are likely to continue to be useful in various future conflicts. Many of the modifications applied to armoured vehicles for the wars will probably remain valuable.

Artillery was effective in the wars and is likely to continue being so in future conflict, as suggested by ongoing fighting in Ukraine, Syria and Iraq. It is likely that unguided artillery will be increasingly complemented by a range of guided shells and rockets, which will include emerging 'man in the loop' indirect-fire, precision-attack capabilities. Direct-fire, indirect-fire and air-delivered precision weapons will probably become ever more important. They will depend on precision ISTAR, and will continue to offer opportunities to reduce civilian casualties and collateral damage.

SOF were valuable in Afghanistan and Iraq, operating both in small parties at long range and integrated with conventional forces conducting COIN efforts. The most important lesson to draw from these experiences relates to the value of integration, not only between SOF and national-intelligence agencies, but equally between SOF and conventional forces. With the end of the war in Afghanistan, the best way to institutionalise this lesson will be through military education and training. SOF will need to adjust their training and capabilities to ensure that they can again operate independently deep in hostile territory. Yet they will also need to retain capabilities developed for both wars, including an improved capacity to integrate ISTAR and intelligence analysis in developing targets, as well as to operate with integral special reconnaissance and supporting infantry.

The success of Iran's Quds Force underlines the value of SOF supporting and influencing indigenous forces in territory that conventional forces cannot or should not reach. It also shows that inter-agency cooperation is just as important to SOF operations as it is to conventional operations.

The wars showed how international forces could successfully raise or co-opt militias. In future, however, it will be essential to make co-opted militias accountable and to deter recidivism or capture by local warlords from the outset.

In both campaigns, airpower gave a decisive asymmetric advantage to US and international forces. Their air superiority was never seriously contested. The conflicts reaffirmed the principle that air forces and armies work best in a land campaign when their actions are fully synchronised.

The use of contractors in stabilisation operations is likely to continue, but it will be crucial for countries employing them to establish a proper framework of command, rules of engagement and legal accountability. This should ensure that contractors' conduct meets the standards for force protection and behaviour of the troops of the country that employs them.

Many of the new developments in battlefield medicine made by the US and its allies are directly relevant to future conflicts. In peacetime, military medical and welfare organisations must be designed to expand to accommodate potential future casualty rates, and to be capable of adapting to new and unforeseen medical and welfare challenges.

In both conflicts, it was essential to rebuild host-nation security forces – firstly to achieve adequate force levels, and then to transition to host-nation security leadership. Initially, capacity-building efforts in Afghanistan and Iraq were under-resourced, and they only received sufficient attention after they were recognised as being equally important to tactical operations. Future efforts to build security capacity should not underestimate the importance of establishing air capability alongside army and police capability. Given the requirement for educated, literate and numerate personnel in air components, it would be wise to begin capacity-building for this most technical of services at the outset.

The wars showed that capacity-building is a core task for all militaries. It would be unwise to allow it to become the preserve of SOF. Embedding mentoring teams in indigenous forces is an effective way of providing active support, coordinating with international forces and building capability and confidence. Institutional reform of defence, security and interior ministries needs to be conducted in parallel with other efforts. Corruption in indigenous forces will often reflect wider corruption in host nations, and is probably best tackled through a comprehensive approach involving political, development and intelligence agencies. It will be crucial for international forces to avoid actions that exacerbate corruption.

CHAPTER FOUR

Learning under fire: military adaptation

The conflicts in Iraq and Afghanistan illuminate the enduring challenges of military adaptation in war. As Williamson Murray puts it:

> War is a contest, a complex, interactive duel between two opponents ... which presents the opportunity for the contestants to adapt to their enemy's strategy, operations, and tactical approach. But because it is interactive, both sides have the potential to adapt to the conflict at every level, from the tactical to the strategic. Thus, the problems posed by the battle space do not remain constant; in fact, more often than not, they change with startling rapidity.[1]

Military adaptation requires the ability to rapidly change equipment, organisation and methods. Discipline and hierarchies are key to the cohesion of armed forces, as are bureaucratic systems for managing logistics, personnel and administration in peace. Yet these structures inhibit flexibility and adaptation in war.

This chapter explains how insurgents rapidly adapted to challenge the intervening forces and how the US and its allies struggled to adapt quickly enough to the unanticipated demands of both wars. Using these examples, it suggests some general lessons for effective military adaptation.

Adaptation 1: insurgents
The Iraqi Sunni insurgency appears to have been largely self-generated from the bottom up, attracting a large number of former Iraqi security personnel, jihadists and cadres of experienced al-Qaeda fighters and organisers. Unencumbered by bureaucracy, they rapidly adopted the technology to deploy improvised explosive devices (IEDs), an adaptation that was accelerated by the transfer of technical knowledge from Lebanese militia Hizbullah and the exploitation of the internet.

Between 2002 and 2005, the Taliban rebuilt its networks in Afghanistan while exploiting grievances with the government in Kabul and its officials. In 2006–07, the Taliban sustained heavy casualties from NATO firepower, and its commanders were relentlessly targeted by NATO special-operations forces (SOF). In response, the group increased the training of its fighters and improved the propaganda it directed at the Afghan people. The Taliban also sought to improve its command and control, increase its networks' resistant to intelligence gathering and conduct targeted assassinations of government officials. However, the adaptation that caused the greatest number of NATO casualties was its increasing use of IEDs, which by 2009 was successfully limiting NATO freedom of manoeuvre, particularly in southern and eastern Afghanistan.

But the adaptations by the Iraqi insurgency were not enough to prevent US and Iraqi forces from degrading al-Qaeda in Iraq or mounting successful counter-insurgency (COIN) operations and SOF attacks. Nor could the adaptations by the Taliban prevent the International Security Assistance Force from clearing most Taliban fighters from major populated areas and key terrain between 2009 and 2012. Despite its repeated proclamations of counter-offensives in each fighting season, the Taliban made few successful attempts to regain territory.[2]

Adaptation 2: Canadian tanks in Afghanistan

Prior to 2006, the Canadian Army had decided to retire its *Leopard* 1 tanks. All armoured vehicles were to be wheeled and lightweight, and the *Leopards* were to be replaced with wheeled *Stryker* Mobile Gun Systems.

Shortly after their deployment to Afghanistan's Kandahar Province in 2006, Canadian troops became involved in much heavier fighting than expected, as the Taliban made extensive use of fortified buildings, trenches and bunkers, as well as IEDs. This climaxed in *Operation Medusa*, an autumn 2006 NATO attack on a well-fortified Taliban position that led to the heaviest fighting Canadian forces had experienced since the Korean War.

Canadian troops had deployed to Kandahar with wheeled light armoured vehicles (LAVs), but found that the vehicles' 25mm cannon was insufficient against Taliban defensive positions. Moreover, the LAV was insufficiently protected and its wheels failed to provide adequate mobility on difficult terrain. The loan of 20 *Leopard* 2 tanks from Germany, followed by a purchase of 80 *Leopard* 2s from Holland, met Canadian forces' need for better firepower, protection and mobility. The deployment of the tanks had a decisive effect on Canadian tactical operations.

Adaptation 3: the United States

The majority of US land forces were ill-prepared for post-conflict stabilisation, as they did not understand Iraqi or Afghan culture and were unfamiliar with the military's role in COIN. In the first part of both stabilisation phases, some US brigades and divisions made good progress. However, the principles of the transition strategy, particularly the withdrawal to large bases outside Iraqi cities, were set in an opposite direction to the principles of COIN.

In late 2003, US forces in Afghanistan began to adapt their tactics and operational design to embrace both COIN and a comprehensive approach, as seen in General David Barno's co-location of his headquarters with the US Embassy and promotion of the Provincial Reconstruction Team concept. In 2004–05, some US Army and US Marine Corps (USMC) commanders in Iraq identified the potential of a COIN approach. These informal, bottom-up adaptations were seen to work in parts in the Iraqi cities of Al-Qaim, Tal Afar and Ramadi.[3] President George W. Bush's decision to replace the transition strategy with the surge and his selection of General David Petraeus to command Multi-National Force–Iraq were both major strategic, top-down adaptations. Petraeus's embrace of the Anbar Awakening was an operational adaptation that decisively shifted the balance of forces in Iraq.

There was also extensive technical adaptation, such as the improvement in US counter-IED capability, which drew on British expertise in this area. Other technical adaptations in response to requests by operational commanders included improvements in battlefield medicine, increased production of unmanned aerial vehicles (UAVs) and the development of mine-resistant ambush-protected (MRAP) vehicles.

During the first half of the Iraq War, these and other technical adaptations were not reaching US troops in Iraq and Afghanistan quickly enough, partly due to an apparent reluctance to shift US armed forces' funding and management effort away from acquiring the weapons and equipment planned for future conventional conflicts. There also appeared to be considerable institutional resistance in some areas, as was reflected in an initial reluctance to buy MRAPs and the US Air Force's unwillingness to shift resources and pilots from manned aircraft to UAVs. As Congress and the four individual services, rather than the Pentagon, controlled equipment budgets, there were opportunities for those who preferred business as usual to create friction and delays.

Secretary of Defense Donald Rumsfeld tried to overcome these roadblocks, but it was Robert Gates, his successor, who accelerated the development, production and deployment of the necessary capabilities. To achieve this, Gates had to overcome entrenched interests and the Pentagon bureaucracy. He found that 'our civilian and military leaders and commanders still lacked urgency and ruthlessness'.[4]

The size and complexity of the Pentagon bureaucracy meant that it would only exhibit the necessary speed and drive if it was given firm top-down direction and leadership by the secretary of defence, the service chiefs and top civilian officials. Gates set up special task forces charged with accelerating the procurement and deployment of MRAPs, UAVs and improved information, surveillance, target-acquisition and reconnaissance capabilities. He also insisted that battlefield evacuation times should be halved, overruling the objections of his medical experts. These initiatives led to a significant increase in MRAP production and deployment, rapid improvement in battlefield medical evacuation and a surge in the deployment of UAVs by a reluctant US Air Force. As Gates later put it:

> Secretary Rumsfeld once famously told a soldier that you go to the war with the army you have, which is absolutely true. But I would add that you damn well should move as fast as possible to get the army you need. That was the crux of my war with the Pentagon.[5]

Adaptation 4: the United Kingdom

The British also struggled to adapt quickly. Although the British Army had considerable experience of COIN from post-war colonial campaigns and Northern Ireland, it had stopped teaching the topic at its staff college in the late 1990s, in favour of instruction on peace-support operations.[6] The UK's up-to-date COIN doctrine was not published until 2009, three years after its US equivalent.

In this and many other areas, it appears that the UK failed to institutionalise key hard-won lessons of Northern Ireland. For example, despite the decisive role of airborne surveillance in Northern Ireland, in Iraq in 2006 the UK had no UAVs capable of flying in the summer heat. The British also failed to improve their tactical intelligence capabilities quickly enough. As a result, in Helmand in 2009, British battalions lacked adequate tactical-intelligence databases.[7]

Nonetheless, the UK applied many counter-IED capabilities developed in Northern Ireland to the campaigns in Iraq and Afghanistan. But, between 2003 and 2006, it fielded an insufficient number of armoured vehicles with adequate protection against IEDS, due in large part to the complex structure of the Ministry of Defence (MoD), which diffused responsibility and accountability. The Iraq Inquiry concluded that:

> the Ministry of Defence was slow in responding to the threat from Improvised Explosive Devices [and] delays in providing adequate medium weight protected patrol vehicles should not have been tolerated. It was not clear which person or department within the Ministry of Defence was responsible for identifying and articulating such capability gaps. But it should have been.[8]

Three years elapsed before public, media and parliamentary pressure on the government led to the June 2006 intervention by defence secretary Des Browne and procurement minister Paul Drayson, which imparted a much-needed sense of urgency. A new vehicle, the *Mastiff*, entered service in December 2006.[9]

It seemed to take the MoD longer to develop the sense of urgency that Gates imparted to the Pentagon. A contributing factor may have been the rapid turnover of UK defence secretaries: there were five between 2001 and 2009, one of whom was also minister for Scotland. During the same period, the US had only two secretaries of defence: Rumsfeld and Gates.

The evidence suggests that for every positive example of Britain's military adaptation, there was an example of its failure to adapt. The MoD's in-house study of the Iraq War concluded that 'in comparison with the US, the UK military was complacent and slow in recognising and adapting to changing circumstances. It took us too long to update our thinking on how to counter the type of insurgency encountered in Iraq.'[10]

Many British officers who fought in both wars often expressed sentiments such as 'we could and should have done better'.[11] There is good evidence that, in important areas, US forces in Iraq changed and adapted faster than the British.[12] As former UK chief of defence David Richards put it:

> Critics say that our long experience in Ulster made us complacent about tackling insurgency elsewhere – a case of 'we've done this in Northern Ireland so we know what to expect and how to deal with it.' As a result of our experience in Ulster, we certainly had a feel for the requirement to keep people with us and work within a political environment. But I think in Iraq, for example, too many British officers would, without realising what they were doing, slip into

a Northern Ireland mindset. Very early on that was an appropriate response when the efficient administration of law and order along the Northern Ireland pattern was required. But once things escalated, we needed to think in new and innovative ways in order to deal with a complex and unique insurgency and the collapse of Iraqi society. That did happen, but maybe it took longer than it should have done.[13]

How to better learn under fire

These examples are but few of the many instances of both successful and unsuccessful adaptation to the changing characters of the wars in Iraq and Afghanistan. They illustrate the importance of leaders and forces innovating and adapting on operations. The adjustments made in Iraq and subsequently applied in Afghanistan show that, although technology can assist with adaptation, the key challenges for adaptation are leadership, culture, and mental and organisational agility.

It was also essential that organisations be prepared to move outside their comfort zones. Some of the resistance to change among the US Air Force and the British Army seems to have been caused by an unwillingness to make culturally uncomfortable decisions and a reluctance to bend themselves out of shape, including by changing their organisational structures and roles, or by prioritising new capabilities at the expense of traditional ones.

Political and military leadership greatly assisted successful adaptation in Iraq and Afghanistan. Bottom-up adaptations could not succeed without the engagement, encouragement and enthusiasm of unit leaders. Top-down adaptation worked best when it was driven by the most senior leaders.

Both military history and management studies strongly suggest that an honest dialogue between front-line, mid-level

Pointers to future conflict: military adaptation

- Both wars showed that adaptation is essential to military success.
- Military organisations and defence ministries often resist necessary change. The key factors that both promote and inhibit adaptation are leadership, culture, and mental and organisational agility.
- Bottom-up adaptation by units on operations must be complemented by top-down encouragement, leadership and direction, particularly in energising inherently conservative military and defence-ministry bureaucracies.
- Leading and encouraging innovation and adaptation is a core task for military commanders and defence officials.

and senior leadership can make organisations significantly more agile and effective. Much of the dialogue within the US Army and the USMC was striking in its candour, not least because much of it occurred in relatively open forums. The dialogue was often self-critical and highly reflective – about what was working and what was not. It embodied a healthy exchange of ideas, not just between tactical practitioners but also between senior officers, company commanders and enlisted troops. Some key senior leaders in the US Army and the USMC seemed confident enough to take critical feedback from their subordinates, supporting good ideas with resources and influence. A British officer who served in Baghdad described the US approach as one of 'brutal frankness'.[14]

CHAPTER FIVE

The utility of force in Afghanistan, Iraq and beyond

While it would be foolhardy to expect future wars to be repeats of Iraq and Afghanistan, the campaigns there provide pointers to the potential future character of conflict, many of which were identified in previous chapters. This chapter takes a wider view, assessing what the wars tell us about the utility of force and the conduct and character of contemporary war, identifying areas in which the United States and its allies could improve the utility of their forces, as well as key implications for military capability.

Iraq and Afghanistan saw clashes of wills between actors seeking to shape events to suit their political aims. The combatants sought to gain and exploit all the advantages they could, often leading to action–reaction dynamics. Attrition, manoeuvre and symmetric or asymmetric military approaches all had roles in the conflicts. These experiences showed the inherent unpredictability of warfare, where the enemy has a vote and may fight to the death to cast it. They demonstrated the factors that Carl von Clausewitz identified as distinguishing war from other activities: the effects of danger, the difficulty of gaining sufficient accurate information and the pervasive presence of friction.[1]

The will of strategic leaders and military commanders at all levels was a key factor in the dynamics of these conflicts. Examples of the unique effects of willpower in these wars include the collapse of the Iraqi Army in March 2003 and the readiness to fight to the death of al-Qaeda members in both countries. There were well-documented instances of effective tactical leadership by US, Coalition and NATO commanders, as well as commanders of Shia militia 'special groups' and Taliban fighters.

In 2006–07, US President George W. Bush demonstrated a will to win in Iraq that had deserted many of his advisers. As commander of US Army Training and Doctrine Command, General David Petraeus played a crucial role in formulating US counter-insurgency (COIN) doctrine; he successfully applied the doctrine in Iraq, changing tactical, operational and strategic dynamics there. Both these efforts required great willpower – firstly, to achieve rapid change in the face of institutional inertia in the US Army and, secondly, in the face of significant political and military friction in Iraq and Washington. It would be wrong to idolise Petraeus – especially as some US units and officers rediscovered the principles of COIN for themselves – but his inspirational and decisive leadership illustrates the enduring importance of the human factor in war.

The utility of force

In a seminal 2005 book, General Rupert Smith proposed that, when engaged in armed conflict, it is essential to assess the utility of force and its potential to alter the situation to achieve desired objectives.[2] In Afghanistan in 2001, US-led forces demonstrated this utility by removing the Taliban regime and significantly reducing the al-Qaeda presence in the country. In 2003 US, UK and Australian forces were effective in rapidly destroying Iraqi

President Saddam Hussein's army and regime. However, their credibility and utility were quickly eroded by the failure to find Iraqi weapons of mass destruction, Iraq's rapid descent into chaos and the abuse of detainees. After Washington decided to rebuild Iraq on a new political model, but applied neither an effective strategy nor sufficient military, political, civilian and development resources to the task, the utility of US force in Iraq declined.

Force had great utility for anti-government insurgents and militias, whose military and political operations threatened the survival of new governments and the success of missions conducted by international forces.

From 'three-block war' to 'n-block war'

The removal of the Taliban government from Afghanistan initially challenged US military and political capabilities; regime change in Iraq was thoroughly planned and drew upon the full range of US military capabilities. Both short regime-change campaigns can be seen as 'linear' conflicts. The subsequent post-conflict stabilisation campaigns were complex and 'non-linear', with many variables interacting in a constantly changing fashion. For instance, in Iraq, there was considerable overlap between militias and organised criminal groups, as well as political and religious extremists and death squads. In both countries, extortion and other crimes often funded insurgent activity.

Military operations took place in an environment that encompassed multiple political, religious, ethnic and economic conflicts. The strategic, operational and tactical levels of conflict often overlapped. A high degree of complexity endured throughout both wars and was felt at every level of command. Petraeus was quoted as saying 'war is not a linear phenomenon; it's a calculus not arithmetic'. Or, as British Lieutenant-General

Graeme Lamb, then deputy commander of Multi-National Force–Iraq (MNF–I), put it in 2007, 'this is as complex as … anything I've ever done … this is three-dimensional chess in a dark room'.[3]

The wars were often described as conforming to the concept of the 'three-block war', defined in 1999 by US Marine Corps General Charles Krulak as:

> Contingencies in which Marines may be confronted by the entire spectrum of tactical challenges in the span of a few hours and within the space of three contiguous city blocks.[4]

This applied to the 2003 British assault on Basra Province early in the war. At one point, the British had besieged Basra city and were attacking it with airstrikes, indirect fire and raids by ground troops, while simultaneously conducting stabilisation operations in the town of Az-Zubayr, as well as arranging the distribution of humanitarian supplies.

An illustration of the complexity of the conflict in Iraq is the range of activities commanded by MNF-I HQ in Baghdad in 2008:

- Attacking Sunni and al-Qaeda insurgents in the Baghdad 'belts'.
- Countering Shia special groups in Baghdad and Basra.
- Building, training and equipping the Iraqi Security Forces.
- Administering the Sons of Iraq militias.
- Mentoring the Iraqi ministries of defence and interior.
- Seeking to persuade the Iraqi prime minister to employ his forces in ways that reinforced rather than inhibited political progress.

- Attempting to reduce friction between Iraqi security forces and Kurdish Peshmerga units by deploying US forces in a peacekeeping role.
- Seeking to avoid the destabilisation of Kurdistan by Turkish strikes against Kurdistan Workers' Party guerrillas in Iraq. This involved sharing intelligence and imagery from unmanned aerial vehicles with Ankara.[5]

Three blocks of war had increased to eight. The conflict in Afghanistan was just as complex. This suggests that these wars were less three-block wars than '*n*-block wars', where *n* was the number of enemy, friendly, inter-agency and neutral or undecided lines of action. This trend is likely to endure.

The wars confirmed that the classic principles of insurgency and counter-insurgency still apply. These include the primacy of politics; addressing the root causes of the insurgency; making progress across all areas of governance and development; retaining legitimacy and operating within the law; and the value of propaganda to insurgents and information operations to counter-insurgents.

Often characterised by British officers as 'nation-building under fire', the prolonged and difficult campaigns in Iraq and Afghanistan were essentially contests for the minds of people: the population, the insurgents and militias and their military and political leaders. This often meant there was a political dimension to military operations.

Twenty-first-century communications, particularly new channels provided by satellite television and social media, increased the interpenetration and interdependence of war and politics. These developments accelerated the transfer of information of varying degrees of accuracy, creating opportunities, risks and threats for all actors and at every level. The character of the conflicts could be illustrated by taking the writings of

Clausewitz, Hobbes, Machiavelli and General Smith, as well as the scripts of television series *House of Cards* and *Game of Thrones* – then dropping them into an industrial shredder.

The role and limitations of the Strategic Corporal

This complexity put additional pressure on military commanders at all levels. Krulak concluded that the outcome of US operations:

> may hinge on decisions made by small unit leaders, and by actions taken at the lowest level ... these missions will require them to confidently make well-reasoned and independent decisions under extreme stress – decisions that will likely be subject to the harsh scrutiny of both the media and the court of public opinion. In many cases, the individual Marine will be the most conspicuous symbol of American foreign policy and will potentially influence not only the immediate tactical situation, but the operational and strategic levels as well. His actions, therefore, will directly impact the outcome of the larger operation; and he will become, as the title of this article suggests – the Strategic Corporal.[6]

The need for a high standard of small-unit leadership persisted throughout both wars, validating the Strategic Corporal concept. But the 'corporals' with the greatest strategic effect were the US and UK commanders who led the abuse of Iraqi prisoners in 2003–04. These tactical actions had an extremely damaging strategic effect, showing that the Strategic Corporal concept cuts both ways.

The episode showed the value of carefully selecting and training small-unit leaders, to better prepare them for their demanding roles in future conflicts. It also demonstrated the value of ethical standards that, without constraining essential fighting spirit and commanders' initiative, create institutional codes of conduct that promote compliance with the law of armed conflict. Commanders must hold the moral compasses of the armed forces and be guided by them.

Legitimacy

Both wars also showed the importance of achieving legitimacy and operating in accordance with the law. As the conflicts unfolded, the US and its allies increasingly recognised that collateral damage and civilian casualties eroded legitimacy and aided the recruitment efforts of militias and insurgents. Therefore, they sought to use force with greater precision and discrimination, adopting highly restrictive rules of engagement and expanding their use of precision weapons.

Despite the legal legitimacy conferred upon them by UN Security Council resolutions, NATO and Afghan-government operations in Afghanistan often struggled to achieve international popular legitimacy. Legitimacy was sometimes an issue for militias and anti-government forces as well. Taliban propaganda and statements increasingly stressed the importance of minimising Afghan civilian casualties, although the conspicuous contradiction between these sentiments and the many civilian deaths from improvised explosive devices (IEDs) and suicide attacks rendered their message almost irrelevant.

Improving the utility of force

Fighting the war as it is, not the war you would like it to be

The evidence suggests that initial stabilisation operations in Afghanistan and Iraq were over-informed by preconceptions based on the previous success of US and NATO forces in Bosnia and Kosovo. This was probably reinforced by the apparent vindication of the Revolution in Military Affairs

(RMA) concept in the rapid toppling of the Taliban and Iraqi regimes. By giving US Secretary of Defense Donald Rumsfeld and others undue confidence that Iraq and Afghanistan could be stabilised with minimal forces, RMA thinking probably contributed to strategic miscalculation. It seems that, between 2002 and 2006, the approach of the US and key allies was partly conditioned by the war that they would have liked to have fought rather than the war as it was.

The political aversion to nation-building of leaders such as Rumsfeld, his political colleagues and other senior officials strengthened their attraction to the RMA, apparently making them reluctant to accept that the wars in Iraq and Afghanistan were different to those envisaged by the concept. This not only influenced the decisions they made about the conduct of both wars, but also predisposed them to persistently emphasise planning for long-term defence capabilities rather than fielding those needed for the wars they were fighting.

Post-conflict stabilisation in both countries revealed a much more complex environment than had been foreseen by the advocates of the RMA. Understanding the situation and the myriad local actors became as important as the narrower understanding of orders of battle and military hardware that had sufficed before 9/11. Much of the successful development of intelligence for COIN saw collection optimised against people and their intentions – intelligence targets that had been de-emphasised by the advocates of the RMA.

There is nothing wrong with armed forces and defence manufacturers seeking to develop new technological capabilities. Indeed, many valuable capabilities have come out of such efforts. But many of the arguments used to advocate the RMA considered the concept in scenarios that played to its strengths, and in ways that minimised the impact of scenarios where RMA capabilities would have less utility.

Formulating and executing strategy

The weaknesses in the formulation and execution of US and UK strategy suggest that governments require coherent and consistent processes for this purpose. A strategy must balance ends, ways and means to produce a plan that can be used by military commanders, diplomats, development agencies and intelligence services, and to formulate an operational-level inter-agency plan. This facilitates the development of tactical plans. There must also be a political strategy to provide the framework for all operational and tactical activities.

It is just as important to have the means to monitor the implementation of strategy. The effectiveness of a strategy must be regularly reviewed, particularly to reassess the utility of the force. This should not only draw on reports from the operational theatre, but also be tested against the assessments of experts who are not part of the government machine.

Integration of all activities at all levels

A central theme, widely applicable in both wars, was the need to fully integrate actions and capabilities. The US and many of its allies conspicuously failed to achieve adequate levels of integration of military with civilian action, both before the invasion of Iraq and for much of the post-conflict stabilisation period.

The value of integrating both military capabilities and action, as well as civilian capabilities and action, was repeatedly shown at the tactical level. By 2010, NATO forces in Afghanistan were demonstrating a well-integrated and advanced approach to clearance operations. Tactical attacks by battalions and brigades, integrating the full range of land and air capabilities at their disposal, were in turn integrated with information operations, reconstruction, development and local political activity. Inter-agency Provincial Reconstruction

Teams had some success in achieving unity of international civilian effort at the provincial and district levels.

This provided a reminder that war and warfare are inherently interdisciplinary activities. Both military commanders and political leaders have key roles in integrating all the capabilities and activities at their disposal. Nations need to be able to fully integrate not just their military efforts, but also intelligence, diplomacy, development and information operations. These initiatives are likely to be as relevant to strategic, operational and tactical success in future conflicts as integrating combined arms and joint capabilities was for military success in the previous decade.

Both wars reinforce the value of unity of effort. For example, in Afghanistan, the Taliban insurgency often achieved a greater political and military unity of effort than the Afghan government and the International Security Assistance Force (ISAF). The US and its allies often had a problematic relationship with the Afghan president. During the US–NATO surge, security operations gained unity of effort from the joint development of a single NATO–Afghan campaign plan, *Operation Omid*. In Iraq and Afghanistan, 'partnering' Iraqi and Afghan units and formations, and embedding teams of advisers within them, promoted unity of effort at the tactical level. Combined tactical operations became increasingly coordinated.

Military implications
Combat is the core military capability
A significant proportion of Western armed forces had achieved results in the Balkans throughout much of the 1990s simply through their presence rather than by fighting. But the Iraq and Afghanistan wars reaffirmed that the core military capability is the capacity to fight. Armed forces that were unable, or whose governments would not allow them, to fight were of little utility

against opponents determined to do so. For some nations, the willingness of enemy fighters in Iraq and Afghanistan to stand, fight and die in a way that Western forces had not experienced since the Korean and Vietnam wars came as a strategic shock.

The wars also confirmed that numbers count: not just numbers of 'boots on the ground', but also extensive training, mentoring and integrating with indigenous armies, militias and police forces. These efforts involved attaching advisers and operational mentors at every level, from defence ministry to company. This applied to the full range of airpower and information, surveillance, target-acquisition and reconnaissance (ISTAR) capabilities, as well as ground-combat forces.

The experiences of the UK contingent in Helmand in 2009 demonstrated the importance of numbers. It had did not have the strength and ISTAR assets to adequately dominate its area of responsibility and protect itself, let alone sustain sufficient pressure on insurgent networks. As a consequence, many of its key bases came to be surrounded by belts of insurgent IEDs. As the British also lacked helicopters, supplies had to be largely delivered by road, requiring major operations to clear IEDs. Both the convoys and the clearance operations led to British casualties. It was only after a US Marine Expeditionary Force reinforced Helmand in the second half of 2009 that they established the force density needed to gain the initiative over the Taliban.[7]

Anti-Western actors

Many violent extremists, insurgents and terrorists will have watched the wars with great interest. The same will be true of countries that have an anti-US, anti-NATO or anti-Western orientation, or whose defence policies require their forces to deter or fight countries that have adopted the Western way of war. These nations include Russia, China, Iran and North Korea. From their point of view, the rapid defeat of the Taliban government and Saddam Hussein's regime would highlight the failure of both leaderships to deter an attack. Neither had a credible capability to oppose the US or its allies with weapons-of-mass-destruction, conventional, unconventional or cyber capabilities. They also lacked effective anti-access/area-denial systems.

Having observed the initial fighting in Iraq and the speed with which the insurgency there arose, such states' defence planners would probably seek to complement conventional armed forces with irregular forces. Both militias and the seed corn of a resistance movement would have a role to play in this approach.

These planners will also have noted the difficulties that the US and its allies encountered in the battle of the narrative. Situations that invite overreaction or increase the chance of civilian casualties create opportunities for propaganda. And, unlike that of most Western countries, such actors' propaganda will not be constrained by the truth.

Anti-Western forces will have seen how cheap, low-tech weapons were able to counter expensive, high-technology US and allied systems. The contest between IEDs and armoured vehicles is a stark example of this. While some capabilities (such as air-defence missiles) are inherently complex and expensive, simpler technologies (such as landmines, sea mines, small arms, rocket-propelled grenades, mortars and artillery shells and rockets) are capable of inflicting casualties on much more advanced and expensive Western forces. Other relevant lessons relate to the value of decentralised organisations and asymmetric approaches. Given the political–military results that Iran achieved in Iraq through Quds Force support for Shia proxies, this combination of diplomatic authority, special forces, clandestine operations and 'train, advise and equip' capabilities appears to be a model with wider applications.

The US and its allies

The forces of the US and its allies are renewing their personnel and equipment, to reconstitute capabilities for the full spectrum of roles required by their defence policies. Many of the advanced conventional weapons they had previously hoped to procure have been cancelled or delayed, so they will have to make hard choices. These decisions are made even harder by a prevailing gloom in the US, NATO and Europe about the utility of force, resulting from the cost and unpopularity of the wars in Afghanistan and Iraq, as well as the difficulty of achieving strategic success in the conflicts.

Some aspects of the wars probably have minimal relevance to future conflicts. For instance, stabilisation operations saw armies deployed to fixed bases rather than living in the field. This allowed for the development of an extensive communications infrastructure, which linked bases into much higher-capacity data networks than may be achievable in future intervention operations. The US and its allies had virtually uncontested use of airpower and the electromagnetic spectrum.

Future expeditionary operations will not necessarily have such advantages. For example, Russian forces have heavily invested in electronic-warfare, air-defence and indirect-fire capabilities. All these have been used to great effect by Russian-supported separatists in eastern Ukraine. Russian army brigades have twice the indirect-fire capability of US and NATO brigades. Russian mortars, gun artillery and artillery rockets out-gun and out-range similar capabilities of US and NATO armies.[8] Beijing has also heavily invested in anti-access/area-denial capabilities, designed to make it more difficult for potential enemies to intervene against China. The country has a wide variety of ways and means to reduce an opponent's air and sea superiority.[9] All these developments challenge the ability of the US and its allies to exploit many key capabilities that provided asymmetric advantage during the Iraq and Afghanistan wars.

A major issue will be attitudes to risk. Achieving rapid military effect will require more risk-taking than was displayed in stabilisation operations, as the 2013–14 French intervention in Mali demonstrated. In that conflict, quickly deployed French troops accepted a far higher risk than did the French contingent in Afghanistan. This is a key potential difference between a possible future conflict and stabilisation operations in Iraq and Afghanistan.

Preparation for expeditionary operations in new theatres will require retraining armed forces, a change of outlook by political leaders and the reconstitution of capabilities that have not been required since the fall of Saddam Hussein. These capabilities include the capacity of land forces to operate against capable conventional armies with credible armour, anti-armour and indirect-fire systems. Air forces will need to regenerate their ability to operate against effective air-defence networks.

Such preparations for future conflict will depend on each nation's defence policy and requirements for its armed forces. Some capabilities fielded for the two wars are likely to be judged as irrelevant for future 'general purpose' forces. Many of the protected patrol vehicles procured for the wars have poor cross-country mobility, meaning that they would have limited utility in future armoured forces.

However, many improvements to the capabilities of the land and air forces that fought in Iraq and Afghanistan are likely to have a wide utility beyond these wars. They include:

- Capabilities to better understand the operational environment, including linguistic, cultural and human-terrain specialists, as well as intelligence analysts. Reflecting the nature of war as a profoundly human activity, these capabilities are centred on people enabled by technology rather than technology alone.

- Surveillance systems and precision weapons, offering options to conduct attacks with fewer civilian casualties and less collateral damage.
- Properly resourced capabilities to hold and interrogate prisoners and detainees that maximise their utility and minimise the chance that they will offer an advantage to the opposition.
- Improved protection for dismounted infantry and armoured vehicles, including advances in casualty evacuation and battlefield medicine. The improved capability to counter IEDs that was fielded during the wars will have wide applications.
- Improved integration between land and air forces and between different national contingents. The best baseline for this will continue to be NATO inter-operability procedures.
- Improved special-operations-forces (SOF) capabilities, including the integration of conventional forces and SOF that was achieved in Iraq and Afghanistan.
- The wide range of unmanned systems, in the air and on the ground, to strengthen the protection of deployed forces, improve surveillance and create new tactical options.

The wars showed that command is a military capability in its own right, requiring the ability to generate layered command and control, including deployable theatre strategic, operational and tactical headquarters. There will be demand for high-level commanders who can understand complexity, deal with a wide variety of political, civilian and military actors, and gain and sustain confidence – particularly with national strategic leaders.

Armed forces need to be capable of manoeuvre, and of gaining an advantage in the battle of the narrative. This requires them to understand the nuances of the operational environment, with a view to influencing local political actors.

To succeed tactically, both the Coalition and ISAF needed the ability to integrate not only traditional combined-arms fire and manoeuvre but also a wide variety of other effects and agencies, including reconstruction, development and information operations. Most Western forces previously saw these capabilities as peripheral, and the reserves were left to generate such capability as existed. US Army Lieutenant-General Michael Vane wrote that:

> Specialized skills are essential for successful operations. The specialized skills required of soldiers today and in the future are articulated ... as New Norms. They include operational adaptability, cultural and language proficiency, negotiation, digital literacy and space knowledge, weapons technical intelligence, and site exploitation. These specialized skills must now become universal tasks.[10]

There is evidence that some armies and air forces are making efforts to do this, but it is unclear whether these initiatives are sufficient. There is less evidence of navies attending to these issues. Such capabilities will only have a decisive effect if they are fully integrated into the armed forces, both in peace and in war. This will require the development and testing, in peacetime, of a gearing mechanism capable of integrating with deployed military headquarters at all levels.

Military intervention after Afghanistan and Iraq

The apparent failure of the US and its allies to achieve their strategic aims in Afghanistan and Iraq has greatly reduced their appetite for military intervention, particularly the deployment of ground troops in a combat role. This shift was underscored by the way that Libya descended into chaos following the successful 2011 NATO intervention in the country.

The Syrian government's use of chemical weapons on its people in 2013 provided another illustration of the West's new aversion to intervention. Although Washington and London had declared the use of such weapons to be a 'red line', the UK Parliament voted against punitive strikes on Syrian government forces. A narrow majority of MPs were unconvinced by the government's case for military intervention to deter further chemical strikes by the regime of Bashar al-Assad. Although the armed forces remain extremely popular among the British public, it appears that, as noted by then-defence secretary Philip Hammond, 'there is a deep well of suspicion about military involvement in the Middle East stemming largely from the experiences of Iraq'.[11] British MPs who voted against their government were not condoning the Assad regime's chemical attacks; they were expressing doubts about the intelligence that was presented, and seeking to avoid being railroaded into rapid action while UN inspectors were still at work in Syria – another parallel with Iraq. Many doubted that the strikes would have any useful effect. The vote showed that important elements of the British media, politicians and people were losing confidence in the utility of force.

The US and its allies have subsequently intervened against violent extremists in Nigeria, the Horn of Africa and Libya. All the campaigns involved the deployment of trainers and advisers to build local military and security capacity, the supply of intelligence and occasional raids by SOF or strikes using unmanned aerial vehicles. These capabilities have been employed against the Islamic State, also known as ISIS or ISIL, in Syria and Iraq – where there has been extensive use of airborne intelligence, surveillance and reconnaissance, as well as precision airstrikes and missile attacks. This would appear to be the post-Afghanistan 'Western Way of War'.

The exception is the 2013 French intervention in Mali, where a jihadist offensive was stopped by attacks using jets and heli-copters. These operations were followed by rapid deployment of SOF, parachute troops and four mechanised battalions from elsewhere in the region, and from mainland France. Had the French not reacted in this way, Mali would have probably fallen to the jihadists.

This campaign suggests that ruling out future direct mili-tary intervention would constrain national options for crisis response, thereby increasing political and military risk. The apparent threat to NATO states posed by Russia's 2014 annex-ation of Crimea, Moscow's subsequent sponsorship of an insurgency in eastern Ukraine and direct intervention with Russian Army tank and artillery battalions led NATO to renew its commitment to collective defence. The centre of gravity of NATO's readiness action plan is the deployment of credible combat-capable forces to Eastern Europe for both exercises and deterrence.

Nonetheless, there is a danger that the intractability of the Iraq and Afghanistan wars may obscure the hard lessons learned in the previous two decades. The 1990–91 US-led intervention in Kuwait – to eject Iraqi forces that had invaded the country – commanded widespread regional and global support, both because of its legitimacy and its rapid success. Between 1992 and 1995, the failure to decisively intervene in the Bosnian civil war prolonged the conflict. NATO's intervention in Kosovo prevented a massacre of Kosovo Albanians, and its subsequent stabilisation operations prevented both conflicts from reigniting.

In Sierra Leone in 2000, the United Kingdom led a national intervention that began by evacuating UK citizens. It rapidly evolved into a direct defence of the town of Lungi against rebels, in which two rebel groups were decisively overmatched. This restored the confidence of a failing UN peacekeeping force. Further displays of force by UK ships, aircraft and troops increased pressure on the rebels. The campaign was a model rapid-intervention operation that transitioned into a long-term UK capacity-building programme.

The rapid deployment to Kabul of a UK-led multinational brigade over the winter of 2001–02 helped the fledgling Afghan authorities restore security to Kabul. There were many success-ful military operations in the wars in Afghanistan and Iraq, but these tactical victories were too rarely converted into strategic effect. The principal factors in this failure were flawed strategic decision-making and poor or inconsistent management of the implementation of strategy.

All this suggests that, despite the attitudinal damage inflicted by the Afghanistan and Iraq wars, the US and its allies still require the policy option of military intervention and its accompanying military capabilities. As David Cameron put it:

> Intervention is hard. War fighting is not always the most difficult part. Often, the state building that follows is a much more complex challenge. We should not be naïve to think that just because we have the best prepared plans, in the real world things can't go wrong. And equally just because intervention is diffi-cult, it doesn't mean that there are not times when it is right and necessary.[12]

CONCLUSION

The experience of the wars in Iraq and Afghanistan suggests that, unless regime change is followed by successful stabilisation, the resulting conditions can be as bad as, if not worse than, those that preceded the campaign. During post-conflict operations in Iraq and Afghanistan, the US and its allies struggled to align ends, ways and means for stabilisation, reconstruction and efforts to achieve the political progress crucial to their strategic objectives. The key weakness was inadequate initial post-conflict stabilisation in both countries, exacerbated by multiple failures to adapt to unanticipated, rapidly changing circumstances.

Too few forces were deployed to provide security in Iraq after regime change. The early, unanticipated deterioration of security and the decision to disband the Ba'ath Party and Iraqi security forces created the conditions for the rise of al-Qaeda, Sunni insurgencies and Shia militias, leading to widespread warfare against dedicated adversaries in a broken country. The initial strategy of quickly transferring responsibility for security to Iraqi forces failed as the country descended into civil war. Until mid-2007, Iraqi insurgents and militias had the initiative.

A comprehensive counter-insurgency (COIN) campaign reversed the decline in security, particularly through the United States' 2007 surge of additional troops into Iraq and co-option of Sunni tribes willing to fight al-Qaeda. This facilitated Iraqi elections and the US withdrawal in 2009, but the underlying tension between Sunnis and Shi'ites remained. The increasingly authoritarian and repressive leadership of Iraqi President Nuri al-Maliki gave rise to an insurgency by the Islamic State, also known as ISIS or ISIL; the defeat of hollowed-out Iraqi forces at Mosul; and another US intervention in Iraq.

In Afghanistan, the initial defeat of the Taliban was followed by inadequate efforts to build state capacity. For the US and its allies, the country was a lower strategic priority than Iraq between 2002 and 2009. During this period, there was often sub-optimal leadership of stabilisation and reconstruction, as well as insufficient international and inter-agency coordination. The Taliban exploited grievances that stemmed from international forces' inadequate understanding of Afghan politics and culture, corruption and predatory behaviour by Afghan officials, as well as civilian casualties and collateral damage.

It was only in 2010 – when security in Iraq improved – that the US and its NATO allies established sufficient force levels and efforts in both COIN and security capacity-building in Afghanistan. They applied many lessons from Iraq, but Afghanistan was a much less developed country, where the political, cultural and reconstruction challenges were even greater. Security only shifted in favour of the Afghan government and NATO at the peak of the 2010–12 surge. After a rapid transition to an Afghan security lead and withdrawal of US and NATO forces from combat operations, problematic Afghan politics and insufficiently developed Afghan forces allowed the Taliban insurgency to persist in many rural areas throughout 2016.

There was often a political dimension to military operations, right down to the tactical level – in line with the concept of 'armed politics'. So understanding the situation, particularly the myriad local politico-military actors, became as important as the narrower understanding of orders of battle and military hardware – as had usually sufficed before 9/11. Both wars show that a modern, inter-agency COIN approach is essential to fighting insurgents. This must be informed by, and influence, politics. The prevalence of intra-state conflict globally suggests that armed forces or defence ministries would take a significant military and political risk were they to remove COIN from their core capabilities (as the US and British armies did before 9/11). Another lesson is that any political strategy must include host-nation national, regional and local governments as independent actors. It must assess the risk that host-nation governments will act in ways that make them part of the problem rather than the solution, due to corruption, politicisation and the existence of parallel structures. Dealing with these issues is likely to require a 'carrot and stick' approach, using both incentives and punitive measures to persuade the government to adjust its behaviour.

Military operations in Iraq and Afghanistan were 'among the people', in urban areas of both countries and in Afghanistan's densely populated Helmand and Kandahar provinces. They were contests for the minds of civilians, insurgents and militias, and their leaders. There was a 'battle of the narrative': a dynamic conflict between insurgent and militia propaganda and the actions and information operations of the US and its allies. Insurgents used the internet and satellite television to get their message across, making the 'propaganda of the deed' an integral part of their operations. Coalition information operations were more constrained and much slower, so the advantage usually lay with the insurgents.

The increasing diversification of the modern media and the speed at which events can be reported and messages formulated and transmitted makes them an ever more important part of the environment in which military operations will be conducted. Future information operations will need to be treated as central to military operations. It will be as important to manoeuvre in the modern information environment as on the ground, at sea or in the air. In some cases, achieving influence will be an equally or even more important objective than destroying enemies or securing terrain. This will be the core business of commanders, but will require properly trained experts. Western forces will need more effective capabilities than those deployed in Iraq and Afghanistan. There may be a role for experts from the marketing and advertising industries, whose approaches have many similarities to information operations.

Previously non-traditional military capabilities such as language and cultural awareness became as important as more traditional military skills. It is likely that these capabilities will be required in future military conflict 'among the people'. The challenge will be to keep the skills alive in peacetime.

In the light of the pervasive twenty-first-century media environment, detainees and prisoners have become totemic issues for all parties to armed conflict and play a major role in the contest for narrative and legitimacy. This highlights the importance of getting the basics right: applying the Geneva Conventions and other relevant legislation, requiring all military personnel to have a thorough understanding of these rules and the values that underpin them. From the outset of operations it is essential to deploy capable prisoner- and detainee-handling organisations and the qualified and trained interrogators required to generate information and intelligence. It will be necessary to use incentives, not only to prevent an insurgency developing within detention facilities, but also to be able to release reformed detainees back to society. It is essential to treat prisoners and detainees as opportunities and potential assets rather than liabilities. There are unlikely to be any short cuts in resourcing this.

Fighting in both wars ranged in scale from low-level fire fights, ambushes and roadside bomb attacks to corps operations featuring several divisions. Tactical ground combat was sometimes as intense as that experienced in the Second World War, Korea and Vietnam. Militias and insurgents in both countries sought to exploit international forces' weaknesses and sensitivity to casualties by using asymmetric approaches and tactics. Insurgents and states that might confront Western forces in future are likely to conclude that these wars show the value of decentralised organisation, asymmetric approaches and cheap and simple ways of producing casualties such as improvised explosive devices (IEDs), landmines, sea mines and low-technology mass-produced light weapons.

As the popularity of the wars declined in all troop-contributing nations, protection and protective equipment became a much higher priority. International forces' casualty levels were reduced by a revolution in battlefield medicine. Countering IEDs became a core activity for all deployed troops. In Afghanistan, all infantry were equipped with handheld detectors and specially organised, advanced counter-IED task forces were fielded.

The principal factor in the eventual tactical success of US forces was rediscovery of the principles of COIN established in earlier wars. These included the primacy of politics, addressing the root causes of the insurgency and making progress across all areas of governance and development. In practice this involved the concentration of sufficient ground troops to provide security for the people through a systematic 'clear, hold and build' approach, measures to control population movement and expanding and decentralising tactical intelligence. Infantry, armour, artillery and combat engineers attacked insurgent strongholds, using combined-arms tactics, complemented by reconstruction, development and information operations. The more operations involved local forces, giving an indigenous face to build empathy with the civil population, the better. Infantry was the most important military capability. The firepower and protected mobility of armoured vehicles were invaluable, wherever the terrain allowed. Tactical integration of airpower into land operations increased throughout the wars.

To reduce collateral damage and civilian deaths, the US and its allies sought to use force with precision and discrimination. This involved highly restrictive rules of engagement and the increasing use of precision bombs, missiles and artillery, linked to increasingly capable intelligence, surveillance, reconnaissance, and command and control. There was greater integration of tactical intelligence with national strategic intelligence and exponential growth in aerial surveillance, particularly by unmanned aerial vehicles (UAVs). Networking these capabilities allowed all-source intelligence analysis to lead the attack of enemy networks. Special-operations forces (SOF) had an increasingly important, but not exclusive, role in this. The full potential of SOF was only realised when their operations were fully integrated with those of conventional forces.

Although the US led both wars, the host-nation governments became increasingly assertive. Considerable international effort was made to build government capacities, particularly their security forces. These initially faltered, but subsequent industrial-scale efforts greatly expanded army, police and intelligence services, albeit at a speed that caused severe growing pains.

In both countries the environment was extremely complex, with the strategic, operational and tactical levels often overlapping. The wars confirmed the 'three-block war' concept, but both wars' additional levels of complexity at their height suggested that they were more like 'n-block wars', where n is the number of lines of operation.

The wars show that although operational plans can correctly anticipate the character of the opening rounds of a campaign, subsequent unexpected events, political developments and action–reaction dynamics can lead to rapid evolution of the character of the conflict in unanticipated directions. During the stabilisation phase the US and its allies often misunderstood the character of the conflicts in ways that reduced their tactical, operational and strategic effectiveness.

The wars showed that successful strategy requires the national alignment of ends, ways and means to achieve strategic objectives, and the enduring importance of strategic leadership. The US failed to do this in the first half of both wars. The alignment of political and military responsibility, authority and accountability was unclear. The US, UK and their allies struggled to adequately integrate their military operations with the rest of their tools, particularly diplomacy and development. The wars confirmed that strategic leadership is more than just the making of strategic decisions: it is also the production of strategic plans and the monitoring and assessment of their implementation. Strategic inter-agency plans allow military commanders, diplomats, development agencies and intelligence services to formulate operational-level inter-agency plans, from which tactical plans can be developed. A political strategy is essential, to provide the foundation for operational and tactical activities. This requires coherent and consistent processes for the formulation of strategy. The effectiveness of a strategy, including the utility of the force being applied, must be regularly assessed and reviewed, drawing on unvarnished reports from the operational theatre, and should be tested both within the machinery of government and against assessments of outside experts.

The wars showed the necessity for military command at levels from the theatre strategic through to the operational and tactical. Tactical action could have strategic effects – both positive and negative, as shown by the damage to US legitimacy inflicted by the abuse of Iraqi prisoners at Abu Ghraib. This not only validated the concept of the Strategic Corporal, but also reinforced the importance of the moral component of military leadership.

Higher commanders had to have highly developed communication and interpersonal skills and the ability to influence a wide variety of actors. They had to gain and sustain the confidence of heads of government and defence ministers, or be replaced. Command became an important military capability in its own right. Commanders needed support by headquarters capable of managing the complexity of operations. Most headquarters were static and able to exploit large quantities of secure bandwidth and processing power, something that will not necessarily apply in future conflicts.

The multinational nature of operations inevitably created frictions, particularly those arising from differing limitations on employment of national contingents, the so-called 'national caveats'. Commanders had a key role in minimising these frictions. NATO acted as a provider of political legitimacy and generator of forces. NATO techniques and procedures helped make national contingents more inter-operable.

A common theme across both wars at every level was the importance of integration. This applied not only to combined-arms military tactics and the considerable improvements in integrating air and land forces and SOF and conventional forces, but also to fully integrating all levers of national power: military, intelligence, diplomatic and development.

Institutionalising future inter-agency cooperation is likely to be an enduring requirement for future conflicts, but will necessitate sustained effort. The relative success of US and NATO military operations in the 1990s was in part the result of facing less capable, modernised and motivated opponents. This led to overconfidence, reinforced by the attractions of the Revolution in Military Affairs (RMA). But the RMA concept had not been adequately tested against insurgents. The initial interventions in Afghanistan and Iraq appeared to confirm the validity of the RMA, but there was insufficient attention to the considerable weaknesses of Taliban and Iraqi forces, who were unable to adapt quickly enough. By giving the US administration false confidence that Iraq and Afghanistan could be stabilised with minimal forces, the RMA misled as much as it informed, contributing to strategic miscalculation. This was exacerbated by the previous neglect of COIN by Western militaries.

As the situation in Iraq deteriorated the RMA seemed to offer little help to the hard-pressed Coalition forces. The surveillance systems that had worked so well against Iraqi conventional forces were of little use against irregulars who blended into the civilian population. Insurgents were often more adaptable than international forces. As both wars continued, some elements of the RMA were adapted, including UAVs, precision weapons and state-of-the-art command-and-control networks. But while these tools were integral to the campaign, they did not define it, suggesting that military concepts and capabilities must be evaluated against the full spectrum of conflict and that armed forces must be educated and trained accordingly.

The US and many of its allies, including the UK, were often too slow to adapt. A significant factor was that defence bureaucracies, such as the Pentagon and the UK Ministry of Defence, wanted to continue with 'business as usual'. This is not a new phenomenon: all bureaucracies exhibit considerable inertia.

Forcing them to recognise that business as usual will not meet the imperatives of war and that they must adapt to the war that they have, rather than the one they want, is a key role of strategic leaders.

The successful adaptations by international forces show that while technology can assist with adaptation, the key enablers and barriers are leadership, culture and mental and organisational agility. Bottom-up adaptation by military units was most successful when complemented by top-down adaptation, direction and support, demonstrating that leading adaptation is a core function of politicians, civilian officials, military leaders and commanders at all levels. Energising military command chains and defence bureaucracies will be an enduring challenge.

The wars show that force had wide utility: for the overthrow of the Taliban and Ba'athist governments, for the conduct of stabilisation operations and for the militias and insurgents that sought to disrupt reconstruction and security. The conflicts confirmed the inherent unpredictability of war, where the enemy has a vote and may fight to the death to cast it. They showed once again that war is a clash of wills between actors seeking to exploit all the advantages they can to shape events to suit their political aims. Attrition, manoeuvre, and symmetric and asymmetric military approaches all had their roles. Although insurgent tactics in both countries were usually asymmetric, for example, international forces exploited their own asymmetric advantages, including control and exploitation of the air, and the employment of armoured vehicles and precision missiles, bombs and rockets.

The ferocity of the armed opposition in both countries was a strategic shock. Against opponents determined to fight, international forces who were unable to fight, or whose governments were not prepared to allow them to fight, were of little utility and often increased military and political friction. The wars reaffirmed that combat is the core military capability and that armed forces should be benchmarked against determined and capable enemies.

In both wars international forces became optimised for COIN, an operational design very different from that needed for rapid-intervention operations in new theatres. They enjoyed largely uncontested control of the air and the electromagnetic spectrum, allowing an elaborate and extensive communications infrastructure with higher-capacity data networks than could be achieved in future intervention operations. They made extensive use of contractors and large operating bases. Extraordinary efforts were made to protect troops, often reducing their utility. These conditions would not necessarily apply in future expeditionary operations, particularly those mounted at short notice, or against a capable state enemy. A particular problem is likely to be overcoming anti-access and area-denial capabilities, especially those that challenge command of the air and the electromagnetic spectrum.

Nevertheless, the likely preponderance of intra-state conflict in future suggests that assuming COIN capabilities will not be needed is risky. Western forces will require a critical mass of understanding, capability and skills to be able to regenerate such capabilities. The US and its allies are seeking to avoid further costly and unpopular interventions by building the security capacities of fragile and failing states to counter insurgency, terrorism or hybrid threats. Experience suggests this should not be solely a military effort, but must be multi-agency from the outset. The credibility and effectiveness of the military component of such assistance will depend on the demonstrable combat capability and understanding of these types of conflict of intervening forces.

The unpopularity of the difficult, extended post-stabilisation operations in Iraq and Afghanistan should not obscure the

considerable military success of the US-led interventions that
began both wars. But the unpopularity of the wars has made it
more difficult for many Western governments to contemplate
the use of force. It is ironic that this is at a time when improvements in capability resulting from these wars, particularly
surveillance and precision weapons, offer options for waging
war more effectively and with fewer civilian casualties and
less collateral damage. Current public, media and political attitudes in the US and its allies largely oppose interventions that
require 'boots on the ground' in combat roles. The evidence
of successful military interventions in the two decades preced-
ing 9/11 suggests that forswearing this capability will greatly
reduce political and military operations to sustain national
interests, deter or reverse aggression and promote stability.

NOTES

Acknowledgements

1 Ben Barry, 'The Bitter War to Stabilise Southern Iraq – British Army Report Declassified', IISS, 10 October 2016, https://www.iiss.org/iiss%20voices/ blogsections/iiss-voices-2016-9143/ october-d6b6/the-bitter-war-to-stabilise-southern-iraq---british-army-report-declassified-953d.

Introduction

1 US Joint Chiefs of Staff, *Doctrine for the Armed Forces of the United States*, 25 March 2013, pp. I-7–I-9, http://www.dtic.mil/doctrine/new_pubs/jp1.pdf.

2 David Richards, *Taking Command* (London: Hachette, 2014), p. 92.

Chapter One

1 For useful accounts of early US SOF and land-force operations in Afghanistan, see Walter L. Perry and David Kassing, *Toppling the Taliban: Air–Ground Operations in Afghanistan October 2001–June 2002* (Santa Monica, CA: RAND Corporation, 2016), available at http://www.rand.org/ pubs/research_reports/RR381.html; and Donald P. Wright et al., *A Different Kind of War: The US Army in Operation ENDURING FREEDOM October 2001– September 2005* (Fort Leavenworth, KS: Combat Studies Institute Press, 2010), http://usacac.army.mil/cac2/csi/docs/ DifferentKindofWar.pdf.

2 'Rumsfeld: Major Combat Over in Afghanistan', 1 May 2003, CNN.com, http://edition.cnn.com/2003/WORLD/ asiapcf/central/05/01/afghan.combat/.

3 Tommy Franks, *American Soldier* (New York: HarperCollins, 2005), pp. 415–16.

4   For a good account of the regime-
    change phase of the war, see Michael
    R. Gordon and Bernard E. Trainor,
    *Cobra II: The Inside Story of the Invasion
    and Occupation of Iraq* (New York:
    Pantheon, 2006). The innovative,
    intelligence-led British operation to
    capture Basra is described well in
    Tim Ripley, *Operation Telic: The British
    Campaign in Iraq 2003–2009* (Lancaster:
    Herrick-Telic Publication, 2004),
    chapters 7–13.

5   For a good account of NATO's campaign
    in Afghanistan in 2006, see David
    Richards, *Taking Command* (London:
    Headline, 2014), chapters 12–14.

6   *Counterinsurgency*, US Department
    of the Army, December 2006, pp.
    2-1–2-2, http://usacac.army.mil/cac2/
    Repository/Materials/COIN-FM3-24.
    pdf.

7   A good account of US and NATO
    operations in Afghanistan is Stanley
    McChrystal, *My Share of the Task: A
    Memoir* (London: Portfolio, 2013),
    chapters 16–20.

8   Author's interviews with NATO
    officials, 2016.

9   'Statement of the Atlantic Summit: A
    Vision for Iraq and the Iraqi People',
    16 March 2003, in Stefan Talmon, *The
    Occupation of Iraq*, Volume II: *The Official
    Documents of the Coalition Provisional
    Authority and the Iraqi Governing Council*
    (Oxford: Hart Publishing, 2012), p. 572.

10 The limitations of the CPA are
    starkly exposed in Hilary Synnott,
    *Bad Days in Basra: My Turbulent
    Time as Britain's Man in Southern Iraq*
    (London: I.B. Tauris, 2008); Rory
    Stewart, *Occupational Hazards: My Time
    Governing in Iraq* (London: Picador,
    2006); and Mark Etherington, *Revolt on
    the Tigris: The Al-Sadr Uprising and the
    Governing of Iraq* (London: Hurst, 2005).

11 For good accounts of *Operation Charge
    of the Knights*, see Peter Mansoor,
    *Surge: My Journey with General David
    Petraeus and the Remaking of the Iraq
    War* (New Haven, CT: Yale University
    Press, 2014), chapter 9; and Jonathan
    Bailey, Richard Iron and Hew Strachan
    (eds), *British Generals in Blair's Wars*
    (Abingdon: Routledge, 2014), chapter
    16.

12 The clearance of Sadr City is best
    analysed in David E. Johnson, M.
    Wade Markel and Brian Shannon, *The
    2008 Battle of Sadr City: Reimagining
    Urban Combat* (Santa Monica, CA:
    RAND Corporation, 2011).

13 For a good analysis of Iraqi politics
    between 2003 and 2011, and the rise
    of Maliki, see Toby Dodge, *Iraq: From
    War to a New Authoritarianism*, Adelphi
    434–435 (Abingdon: Routledge for the
    IISS, 2012).

14 For a useful analysis, see David
    Kilcullen, *Blood Year: Islamic State and
    the Failures of the War on Terror* (London:
    Hurst, 2016), chapters 8–9.

15 A variety of terms have been used
    to describe the ways and means by
    which both international forces and
    insurgents sought to achieve this.
    The terminology used by the US
    and NATO can be bewildering to
    the uninitiated, and it often changed
    during the 13 years of conflict. This
    book uses a modified version of a
    recent NATO definition of information
    operations as a military function to
    'create desired effects on the will,
    understanding and capability of
    adversaries, potential adversaries and
    other [approved] parties in support of
    [mission] objectives'. See NATO, *Allied
    Joint Doctrine for Information Operations*,
    November 2009, available at https://
    publicintelligence.net/nato-io/.

16 Author's observation, HQ ISAF Joint Command, June 2013.

17 H.R. McMaster, 'Effective Civilian–Military Planning at the Operational Level: The Foundation of Operational Planning', in Michael Miklaucic (ed.), *Commanding Heights: Strategic Lessons from Complex Operations* (Washington DC: Center for Complex Operations, 2009), pp. 105–14, http://cco.ndu.edu/Portals/96/Documents/books/commanding-heights/commanding_heights.pdf.

18 Author's interviews, 2009–10.

19 Andrew Mackay and Steve Tatham, *Behavioural Conflict: Why Understanding People and Their Motives Will Prove Decisive in Future Conflict* (Saffron Walden: Military Studies Press, 2011).

20 Emile Simpson, 'America Must Leave the Defeat of Isis to Local States', *Financial Times*, 11 September 2014.

21 Carter Malkasian, *War Comes to Garmser: Thirty Years of Conflict on the Afghan Frontier* (London: Hurst, 2013).

Chapter Two

1 Readers may find it useful to refer to the definitions of levels of command on p. 14.

2 The Iraq Inquiry Report (also known as the Chilcot Report), published on 6 July 2016, and supporting documents are available at http://www.iraqinquiry.org.uk/.

3 Iraq Inquiry Report, 'Executive Summary', p. 91.

4 Private conversations with UK officials, 2016, and analysis of House of Commons Defence Committee report 'Afghanistan – Camp Bastion Attack', 28 March 2014, http://www.publications.parliament.uk/pa/cm201314/cmselect/cmdfence/830/83002.htm.

5 Ben Barry, 'The Bitter War to Stabilise Southern Iraq – British Army Report Declassified', IISS, 10 October 2016, https://www.iiss.org/iiss%20voices/blogsections/iiss-voices-2016-9143/october-d6b6/the-bitter-war-to-stabilise-southern-iraq---british-army-report-declassified-953d.

6 George Bush, *Decision Points* (New York: Crown, 2010), p. 268.

7 *Ibid.*, pp. 363–75.

8 Iraq Inquiry Report, section 10.4, p. 9.

9 Iraq Inquiry Report, section 9.8, p. 481.

10 John Chilcot's public statement, 6 July 2016, http://www.iraqinquiry.org.uk/the-inquiry/sir-john-chilcots-public-statement/; Iraq Inquiry Report, 'Executive Summary', pp. 124–5.

11 Iraq Inquiry Report, section 9.8, p. 502.

12 Author's interviews, 2009–10.

13 Richard Dannatt, *Leading from the Front: An Autobiography* (London: Corgi, 2010).

14 Iraq Inquiry Report, section 10.4, p. 533.

15 Iraq Inquiry Report, section 10.1, p. 95.

16 Hilary Synnott, *Bad Days in Basra: My Turbulent Time as Britain's Man in Southern Iraq* (London: I.B. Tauris, 2008), p. 252.

17 See Peter Ricketts, 'National Security in Practice: The First 18 Months of the National Security Council', address at the IISS, 30 November 2011, http://www.iiss.org/en/events/events/archive/2011-1092/november-75d8/national-security-in-practice-the-first-

18-months-of-the-national-security-council-123b; David Richards, *Taking Command* (London: Headline, 2014), chapter 16.

18 Robert Gates, *Duty: Memoirs of a Secretary at War* (New York: Alfred A. Knopf, 2014), p. 206.

19 See Tommy Franks, *American Soldier* (New York: HarperCollins, 2005); Stanley McChrystal, *My Share of the Task: A Memoir* (London: Portfolio, 2013); Richards, *Taking Command*; and George W. Casey, Jr, *Strategic Reflections* (Washington DC: National Defense University Press, 2012).

20 For examples of this in a US brigade, see Daniel P. Bolger, *Why We Lost: A General's Inside Account of the Iraq and Afghanistan Wars* (Boston, MA: Eamon Dolan, 2014), pp. 352–6.

21 The different approaches are vividly illustrated by accounts of two provincial governance coordinators of the British role in Amarah during the 2004 Shia uprising. See Rory Stewart, *Occupational Hazards: My Time Governing in Iraq* (London: Picador, 2007); Mark Etherington, *Revolt on the Tigris: The Al-Sadr Uprising and the Governing of Iraq* (London: Hurst, 2005); and Richard Holmes, *Dusty Warriors: Modern Soldiers at War* (London: Harper, 2006).

22 Carl Bildt, *Peace Journey: The Struggle for Peace in Bosnia* (London: Weidenfeld & Nicolson, 1998); Paddy Ashdown, *Swords and Ploughshares: Bringing Peace to the 21st Century* (London: Orion, 2007).

23 NATO, 'A "Comprehensive Approach" to Crises', 21 August 2014, http://www.nato.int/cps/en/natohq/topics_51633.htm.

24 US Department of Defense, *Decade of War*, Volume 1: *Enduring Lessons from the Past Decade of Operations*, J7 unclassified internal publication, p. 11, available at http://smallwarsjournal.com/blog/analysis-of-a-decade-at-war.

25 Carter Malkasian, *War Comes to Garmser* (Oxford: Oxford University Press, 2015), p. 85.

26 Iraq Inquiry Report, section 10.4, p. 529.

27 Author's interviews, 2009–10.

28 Author's interviews with US and UK officers and civilian officials, 2009–10.

Chapter Three

1 For an account of a British company completely surrounded by deep belts of IEDs, see Richard Streatfeild, *Honourable Warriors: Fighting the Taliban in Afghanistan* (Barnsley: Pen and Sword, 2014).

2 Peter Mansoor, *Surge: My Journey with General David Petraeus and the Remaking of the Iraq War* (New Haven, CT: Yale University Press, 2014), p. 168.

3 Author's interviews with former Secret Intelligence Service senior officials, 2014.

4 See Sean Naylor, *Not a Good Day to Die: The Untold Story of Operation Anaconda* (London: Michael Joseph, 2005).

5 US Army, *The US Army Capstone Concept*, 19 December 2012, p. 11, http://www.tradoc.army.mil/tpubs/pams/tp525-3-0.pdf.

6 Author's observations, HQ UK Task Force, Helmand, June 2009.

7 Author's observation, HQ NATO International Joint Command, Kabul, June 2013.

8 Author's observations, Helmand and Kandahar, June 2009.

9 See Daniel P. Bolger, *Why We Lost: A General's Inside Account of the Iraq and Afghanistan Wars* (Boston, MA: Eamon Dolan, 2014), pp. 197–8.

10 Author's interviews, 2009–10.

11 Baha Mousa Inquiry, *The Report of the Baha Mousa Inquiry*, vol. 2 (London: HM Stationery Office, 2011), paragraph 7.208, https://www.gov.uk/government/uploads/system/uploads/attachment_data/file/279209/1452_ii.pdf.

12 Stanley McChrystal, *My Share of the Task: A Memoir* (London: Portfolio, 2013), p. 201.

13 Mansoor, *Surge*, pp. 151–4.

14 Author's observations, Kabul, 2013.

15 Author's interviews, 2009–10.

16 For a comprehensive account of British development of battlefield medicine in 2003–09, see the evidence given to the Iraq Inquiry by Lieutenant-General Louis Lillywhite, the UK military surgeon general, available at http://www.iraqinquiry.org.uk/media/95370/2010-07-20-Transcript-Lillywhite-S3.pdf.

17 For a vivid but realistic account of the medical treatment of a seriously injured British infantry officer in Afghanistan and the UK, see the autobiographical novel *Anatomy of a Soldier*. The author lost both legs in an IED blast in Helmand. Harry Parker, *Anatomy of a Soldier* (London: Faber & Faber, 2016).

18 See Mark Urban, *Task Force Black: The Explosive True Story of the SAS and the Secret War in Iraq* (London: Little, Brown, 2010). This account of Special Air Service (SAS) operations in Iraq contains much tactical detail of the force's raids and combat. However, it appears that some of the author's sources were furthering personal agendas, reflecting tensions within the SAS.

19 JSOC's interrogation operations are described in McChrystal, *My Share of the Task*, p. 202. See also Ben Barry, 'Stanley McChrystal, Special Forces and the Wars of 9/11', *Survival: Global Politics and Strategy*, vol. 55, no. 5, October–November 2013.

20 Robert Gates, *Duty: Memoirs of a Secretary at War* (New York: Alfred A. Knopf, 2014), p. 267.

21 Carter Malkasian, *War Comes to Garmser: Thirty Years of Conflict on the Afghan Frontier* (London: Hurst, 2013), p. 87.

22 Author's observations, Afghanistan, 2009.

23 This is well described in Jonathan Bailey, Richard Iron and Hew Strachan (eds), *British Generals in Blair's Wars* (Abingdon: Routledge, 2014), chapter 16.

24 For a vivid account of a British OMLT, see Patrick Hennessey, *The Junior Officers' Reading Club: Killing Time and Fighting Wars* (London: Allen Lane, 2009).

25 See Malkasian, *War Comes to Garmser*, pp. 206–7.

26 Insight from British Army Iraq Lessons Conference, January 2010.

27 Author's discussions with Task Force–Shafafiyat.

Chapter Four

1   Williamson Murray, *Military Adaptation in War: With Fear of Change* (Cambridge: Cambridge University Press, 2011), chapter 1.
2   Analysis based on various sources, including Antonio Giustozzi, 'Military Adaptation by the Taliban, 2002–2011', in Theo Farrell, Frans Osinga and James A. Russell (eds), *Military Adaptation in Afghanistan* (Stanford, CA: Stanford University Press, 2013), pp. 242–62.
3   James Russell, *Innovation, Transformation and War: Counterinsurgency Operations in Anbar and Ninewa Provinces, Iraq, 2005–2007* (Stanford, CA: Stanford University Press, 2010).
4   Robert Gates, *Duty: Memoirs of a Secretary at War* (New York: Alfred A. Knopf, 2014), p. 116.
5   *Ibid.*, p. 148. The chapter 'Waging War on the Pentagon' is an interesting study of leadership of adaptation.
6   Identified in British Army analysis of stabilisation operations in Iraq. See Ben Barry, 'The Bitter War to Stabilise Southern Iraq – British Army Report Declassified', IISS, 10 October 2016, https://www.iiss.org/iiss%20voices/blogsections/iiss-voices-2016-9143/october-d6b6/the-bitter-war-to-stabilise-southern-iraq---british-army-report-declassified-953d.
7   Author's observations from visits of UK battalions in Helmand, June 2009.
8   Public statement by John Chilcot, chairman of the UK Iraq Inquiry, 6 July 2016, http://www.iraqinquiry.org.uk/the-inquiry/sir-john-chilcots-public-statement/.
9   Iraq Inquiry Report, section 14.2, pp. 229–34.
10 UK Ministry of Defence, 'Iraq Study Team Observations', https://www.gov.uk/government/uploads/system/uploads/attachment_data/file/16787/operation_telic_lessons_compendium.pdf.
11 Author's interviews, 2009–10.
12 Author's assessment based on his work on the lessons of Iraq for the British Army, 2009–10.
13 David Richards, *Taking Command* (London: Headline, 2014), p. 78.
14 Author's interview, 2009.

Chapter Five

1   See Carl von Clausewitz, *On War*, ed. and trans. Michael Howard and Peter Paret (Princeton, NJ: Princeton University Press, 1989), pp. 16–18.
2   Rupert Smith, *The Utility of Force: The Art of War in the Modern World* (London: Allen Lane, 2005).
3   Peter Mansoor, *Surge: My Journey with General David Petraeus and the Remaking of the Iraq War* (New Haven, CT: Yale University Press, 2014), p. 223.
4   Charles C. Krulak, 'The Strategic Corporal: Leadership in the Three Block War', *US Marine Corps Gazette*, vol. 83, no. 1, January 1999.
5   Drawn from Michael Gordon and Bernard Trainor, *The Endgame: The Inside Story of the Struggle for Iraq, from George W. Bush to Barack Obama* (New York: Pantheon, 2012), chapter 32.
6   Krulak, 'The Strategic Corporal'.
7   Author's research, Helmand, 2009.

8   See John Gordon IV et al., *Comparing U.S. Army Systems with Foreign Counterparts: Identifying Possible Capability Gaps and Insights from Other Armies* (Santa Monica, CA: RAND Corporation, 2015), chapter 3.

9   See David C. Gompert, Astrid Cevallos and Cristina L. Garafola, *War with China: Thinking through the Unthinkable* (Santa Monica, CA: RAND Corporation, 2016).

10 Michael A. Vane, 'New Norms for the 21st Century Soldier', *Military Review*, July–August 2011, pp. 16–24.

11 Robert Winnett, 'Syria Crisis: No to War, Blow to Cameron', *Telegraph*, 29 August 2013, http://www.telegraph.co.uk/news/worldnews/middleeast/syria/10275158/Syria-crisis-No-to-war-blow-to-Cameron.html.

12 David Cameron, 'PM Statement on the Iraq Inquiry, 6 July 2016', https://www.gov.uk/government/speeches/pm-statement-on-the-iraq-inquiry-6-july-2016.

INDEX

Adelphi books are published eight times a year by Routledge Journals, an imprint of Taylor & Francis, 4 Park Square, Milton Park, Abingdon, Oxfordshire OX14 4RN, UK.

A subscription to the institution print edition, ISSN 1944-5571, includes free access for any number of concurrent users across a local area network to the online edition, ISSN 1944-558X. Taylor & Francis has a flexible approach to subscriptions enabling us to match individual libraries' requirements. This journal is available via a traditional institutional subscription (either print with free online access, or online-only at a discount) or as part of our libraries, subject collections or archives. For more information on our sales packages please visit www.tandfonline.com/librarians_pricinginfo_journals.

2017 Annual Adelphi Subscription Rates			
Institution	£634	$1,201 USD	€1,013
Individual	£242	$413 USD	€330
Online only	£599	$1,051 USD	€886

Dollar rates apply to subscribers outside Europe. Euro rates apply to all subscribers in Europe except the UK and the Republic of Ireland where the pound sterling price applies. All subscriptions are payable in advance and all rates include postage. Journals are sent by air to the USA, Canada, Mexico, India, Japan and Australasia. Subscriptions are entered on an annual basis, i.e. January to December. Payment may be made by sterling cheque, dollar cheque, international money order, National Giro, or credit card (Amex, Visa, Mastercard).

For a complete and up-to-date guide to Taylor & Francis journals and books publishing programmes, and details of advertising in our journals, visit our website: http://www.tandfonline.com.

Ordering information:
USA/Canada: Taylor & Francis Inc., Journals Department, 530 Walnut Street, Suite 850, Philadelphia, PA 19106, USA. UK/Europe/Rest of World: Routledge Journals, T&F Customer Services, T&F Informa UK Ltd., Sheepen Place, Colchester, Essex, CO3 3LP, UK.

Advertising enquiries to:
USA/Canada: The Advertising Manager, Taylor & Francis Inc., 530 Walnut Street, Suite 850, Philadelphia, PA 19106, USA. Tel: +1 (800) 354 1420. Fax: +1 (215) 207 0050. UK/Europe/Rest of World: The Advertising Manager, Routledge Journals, Taylor & Francis, 4 Park Square, Milton Park, Abingdon, Oxfordshire OX14 4RN, UK. Tel: +44 (0) 20 7017 6000. Fax: +44 (0) 20 7017 6336.